Advance Praise

"In *Beyond One*, Jennifer Bingham H[illegible] the choice to have more than one chi[illegible] book covers the variety of issues, some humorous, some not, which arise with the birth of a second child. Her insights and personal anecdotes are amusing and helpful. A must-read for those considering another baby!"

—Sal Severe, Ph.D.,
author of *How to Behave So Your Preschooler Will, Too!*

"I wish Jennifer Bingham Hull had written *Beyond One* when my second baby was born, and I suddenly realized I was outnumbered. Then I would have understood why it felt as though I had added not just one baby, but one thousand. Every mother even thinking about adding a little sister or brother to the mix should read this book. And quickly, too, because someone's bound to scribble on it when Mommy's not looking."

—Jen Singer,
author of *14 Hours 'Til Bedtime*

"Having two children is often expected in American culture, but rarely given the kind of attention that it deserves. How do we grow into a family and yet maintain a life as women, as men, as individuals? *Beyond One* asks these questions. This personal account of growing a family and getting a life is filled with rich narratives. Jennifer Bingham Hull makes it real! *Beyond One* is an important and extremely readable book. Anyone contemplating having a second child should read it."

—Rebecca L. Upton,
Assistant Professor of Anthropology, DePauw University

BEYOND ONE

Growing a Family and Getting a Life

Jennifer Bingham Hull

SEAL PRESS

BEYOND ONE

Growing a Family and Getting a Life

Some of the material in this book has appeared previously in *Brain, Child* and *Parenting* magazines.

Published by
Seal Press
An Imprint of Avalon Publishing Group Incorporated
1400 65th Street, Suite 250
Emeryville, CA 94608

Cataloging-in-publication data has been applied for.

ISBN 1-58005-104-9

9 8 7 6 5 4 3 2 1

Cover design: Gia Giasullo, studio eg
Interior design: Margaret Copeland/Terragrafix
Printed in Canada by Transcontinental Printing
Distributed by Publishers Group West

To my mother,
who makes me laugh,

and Bill,
who makes it all possible.

somewhere i have never travelled,gladly beyond . . .

—e.e. cummings

Table of Contents

INTRODUCTION

Taking the Leap

I'm an unlikely candidate for mothering more than one child. Growing up, I seldom played with dolls. I avoided babysitting and turned down a job as a camp counselor. As an adult, I did six months of therapy before deciding to have my first daughter, Isabelle. I was thrilled about my first baby. But when she was nine months old and a friend asked whether I wanted another child, I answered, "Absolutely not!" After months of sleep deprivation, diaper duty, and midnight meltdowns, one child seemed more than enough. I couldn't imagine how I'd preserve my sanity, much less a sense of self, with two.

A few generations ago, my response might have shocked. One-child families were relatively rare, singletons an oddity. Today, though, factors such as women's high participation in the workforce and the availability of birth control have made having a second much less automatic. Once unusual, single-child families are now the fastest-growing family unit in America, having increased from 9.6 percent in 1976 to more than 17 percent in 1998. In New York City, they've become the norm. Even in that bastion of big families, Italy, more women are stopping at one.

The trend toward later childbearing explains some of this shift. However, some women are also doing what was once unthinkable: choosing to have only one child. And there is good reason. A smaller family means less laundry, more mobility, lower expenses, and less responsibility. It's far easier to work and have time for your spouse with one. Furthermore, despite the popular belief that only children end up spoiled and lonely, studies find that they do just fine. Mothers like author Anita Diamant speak positively of having one:

> For me, it was a choice. My husband and I agreed that three is cozy and complete. My daughter has asked, from time to time, why she has no brother or sister, and I have answered with the line (attributed to Brooke Astor's mother) about stopping at perfection. Emilia likes to hear that. Who wouldn't? . . .
>
> I don't think being an only child caused her any suffering. Like most onlys, she thrived, excelled in verbal skills and charming adults, but is otherwise virtually indistinguishable from children who have siblings. It's good for me, too. I love my work, I see my friends, and I've been able to give my daughter my undivided attention. My store of patience, such as it is, is at her disposal. I know I'm being the best mommy I can be, and I'm quite sure I wouldn't be able to say that if we'd had more than one.

Stopping with one, I'd be in good company. Half of the women in my baby group stopped after one. Many accomplished women have been mothers of singletons, including Margaret Mead, Hilary Rodham Clinton, Sigourney Weaver, and some of my favorite writers. Erica Jong has one child. So do Alice Walker and *The Artist's Way* author Julia Cameron.

In contrast, a glance at my bookshelves seemed to reveal that having two or more kids is a recipe for disaster. Mother-of-four Tillie Olsen penned one of the most depressing, if stunning, books on motherhood's toll on creativity with *Silences*. Betty Friedan got so frustrated staying home with three that she launched a revolution. Sylvia Plath had two toddlers when she put her head in the oven. Alice Walker's words rang in my ears: "With one, you can move. With more than one, you're a sitting duck."

So I was set on one as Isabelle approached her first birthday. No one in my family was pressuring me to produce more, least of all my husband, who by then had lived with the bitch in the house for almost a year. A doting grandmother, Bill's mother had even surprised me by suggesting that we might want to quit while we were ahead. And she had a point. Except for her lousy sleep habits, Isabelle was perfect. Why push our luck?

Then Isabelle turned one, I got some help, a bit more sleep, and caught the second-baby bug. Bill wasn't so sure about having another, vividly recalling the hysterical, exhausted woman who'd thrown a pot at his head during Isabelle's first week. Why go backwards, he asked, when our toddler hadn't even gotten through potty training and was still often waking us at night? And what about all those logical arguments for having one?

I might have quoted Pascal, who said: "The heart has its reasons which reason knows nothing of." For having another child is an emotional affair. But my husband is a law professor, so I made my case. I explained that the ratio of one child to two, three, and sometimes more adults, depending on whether Grandma was in town, felt lopsided. I wanted to see kids tumbling on the grass together. I wanted to hear another pair of tiny feet padding down the hall. And, while three kids would raise significant financial issues—the government estimates that it can cost a middle-class couple as much as $250,000 to raise a child, not including college—we could afford two. Space would be tight but our house would do, especially if they could share a room. It's a dice roll. Jimmy Carter got Billy. Abel got Cain. Yet I wanted Isabelle to have a sibling, knowing how much I value my two brothers. Most of all, I thought having another child would be fun.

My serious academic could not relate. Fun still seemed a distant and unlikely prospect with one child, much less two. Bill loves and respects his sister, but they were not particularly close growing up, their personalities almost polar opposites, with Bill introverted and his sister extroverted. Since Isabelle's birth, he'd been teaching classes by the seat of his pants and had put off much of his academic writing. Bill also knew that with a second we'd have the same deal we'd had with our first: shared parenting. And this time, he knew what that meant.

Women usually get their way on family size. Still, I was surprised when, soon after this conversation, Bill agreed to try for another child. Second thoughts on siblings? Fun-filled visions of a family of four? Well, no, he explained. It hadn't been any of that. Bill had thought it over and decided that, in the long run, children would be one of his greatest legacies, worth any short-term sacrifice. It was an argument I hadn't even considered.

And so we made the leap, and not long after, I sat balancing our toddler to one side of my large belly, reading *Angelina's Baby Sister*. As I read to Isabelle, however, I remained distracted by concerns of my own. These were not the questions of my first pregnancy—about pacifiers and sleep schedules. Of course, I worried about managing two, but most of my questions were more personal and profound. I now knew that children change your life. Who, I wondered, would I be beyond one—not just as a mother, but as a woman, writer, wife, and friend?

Now an experienced parent, I felt confident caring for a child. Yet I also knew what that really meant. Would I be able to address my own needs once outnumbered by little people? Could I love two? Our parenting partnership had been key in my decision to conceive a second. But how would fifty-fifty function with a bigger family? Would we fight as much as we had after Isabelle's birth to establish the rules of the game?

And what about work? My first had cured me of any illusions of churning out magazine articles with a baby sleeping by my side, and as a result, I already had help. I've been a writer for twenty years and planned to continue working after a second. However, my office is in the house, and I'd discovered from Isabelle both the benefits and the perils of working at home. How would I juggle writing with another child?

And what about my personal life? Would I ever have coffee with a friend again? Read a novel? See a movie? What about that bulging belly and that big number on the scale? Would I ever fit into my jeans again? Feel attractive? Have time for—or even want to have—sex?

Back then, when this land beyond one was still theoretical, I felt like a worrywart. Now I see how legitimate my concerns were. While most research has focused on the first child's effect on family life, those who have examined the second's have found its impact in some ways more life changing and difficult. For the couples profiled in Arlie Hochschild's *The Second Shift*, the second child provoked a crisis, especially for mothers, as husbands failed to share the extra load. Studying twenty-five dual-career couples with two small children, anthropologist Rebecca Upton found many parents overwhelmed by the new demands of family life. Nearly 27 percent of the mothers and 17 percent of the fathers had stress levels so high that they were offered referrals for consultations in Robert Stewart's research on the impact of the second child on 41 American couples. Studies from around the world have noted a decline in mothers' well being as family size increases, with one survey finding women's life satisfaction dropping to an all-time low in the year after the arrival of a second child.

With one child, a mother often can manage to do it all. Making dinner after getting home from work with a toddler trying to "help" and a baby on the hip is another matter. The arrival of a second child often brings a critical change in family roles. For men, it's a time for increased family involvement, "the first made us a family, the second made me a father" being the much-repeated male refrain. Women, though, often face significant work-family conflicts. As Upton's study notes, while most paid professional women return to full-time work after the first child, more than half change to part-time employment or take a leave after the second. Ann Crittenden notes the clash many women face between work and the next child in *The Price of Motherhood:*

> The most popular form of family planning in the United States and other wealthy countries—two children, spaced not too far apart—is incompatible with most women's careers. Even if a new mother and her employer can cope with one child, the second baby is often the final straw. The most sympathetic employers can prove surprisingly resistant to the second baby.

These changes and pressures make for a critical marital crossroads. Studies find the birth of a second child commences the most difficult year in a marriage. Overwhelmed by extra work, many wives seek a more equitable division of parenting duties. Yet mothers often fail to get it, a fact that contributes to what Hochschild calculated as an extra month of work a year for women. This "second shift" negatively affects marriages and thus men too. In contrast, women whose husbands share domestic duties with two, such as those portrayed in Francine Deutsch's *Halving It All: How Equally Shared Parenting Works*, while making career sacrifices, generally do much better.

Yet although the majority of American mothers has two or more children, little has been written on these issues. Isabelle at least had *Angelina's Baby Sister*. Most adult parenting books are for first-time mothers or address children's needs solely; pregnancy alone takes up an entire bookstore shelf. However, while every twinge had fascinated me with my first, my main interest in my second pregnancy was finishing it; I couldn't get myself to even open *What to Expect When You're Expecting.*

A magazine editor sent me a long article about the logistics of bathing a toddler and a baby together. Up to my ears in bath bubbles already, I couldn't read it. The few guides that did discuss having a second child focused on the pregnancy and first few months. I knew, from my first, that the early days would be challenging. Yet when, if ever, would things get easier?

When the general parenting guides do turn their attention to a second child, they focus so much on sibling rivalry that it sounds like the firstborn is having the baby. Though they offered me some good tips, their perspective seemed negative and narrow. Most of my friends' kids got along fine. And hadn't I conceived a second in part because of my own fond memories of playing with my brother? Studies find that the vast majority of siblings value their relationship considerably, both as older children and as adults. Why, then, so many scary stories about sibling strife? And why didn't they note what my own mother—who raised two kids three years apart and then a third separately much later—cited as the joy of parenting two at a time: having children who can play together? Providing a sibling is one of the main reasons parents venture beyond one. Yet the books presented lists of things to do to make up to the first for having a second, as if it were some great crime.

Life with two, I knew, would be busier than ever. However, the parenting tomes only added to my to-do list. Mom, as a human being, with interests and needs of her own, was barely mentioned. Dad, who common sense suggested would be more essential than ever, was often nowhere to be found. And as for the relationship between them? Even the memoirs dared not touch what studies indicated should be of great concern: the marital tie. Not surprisingly, the great mommy memoirs—*Operating Instructions, The Lunch-Box Chronicles, American Mom*—were all written by single women. Go to dinner with any mother, and husbands are the main course. On marriage, however, mommy writers are generally mum.

I wanted to remain close to my firstborn but wasn't planning to make her a special photo album, much less complete an illustrated book, or borrow a baby for us to practice together as the guides suggested. Presumably, other real-life mothers don't have time for these things either, or if they do, the activities don't help. Research shows a marked deterioration in the relationship between the older sibling and the mother after a second child's birth. How, I wondered, could I preserve closeness with Isabelle after the baby arrived? My firstborn had favored me so much that she'd practically sabotaged my agreement with Bill to share parenting. Now I was expecting another girl. Would it be one for you and one for me—or two on my lap and Daddy on the outs?

I wanted a friend who could answer these questions. But most Mommy-and-me groups are for first-timers. While it had been easy to lure a mom with one baby to Starbucks, my mother-of-two friends were too busy to socialize. During the brief exchanges we did have at the park, they contradicted one another. Two kids, it seemed, were anywhere from one and a half to ten times the work. And I couldn't get myself to ask whether they still had sex with their husbands or had battered their mates with any kitchenware.

So instead, I watched from afar as they dashed after their little ones at the park, and slung baby and toddler at the preschool pickup, busier than any chief executive I ever interviewed while reporting at *The Wall Street Journal.*

Watching, I wondered.

Who were they?

And who would I be, beyond one?

Room Service

I gave birth to both of my children at Jackson Memorial Hospital in Miami. The same obstetrician delivered both babies. Bill attended both births. Each time the sky parted, and a beautiful baby girl with velvety skin and cherry lips emerged. But the woman who gave birth to the first baby was almost unrecognizable from the one who delivered the second.

When, during my first hospital stay, the obstetrician told us he'd have to do a cesarean section, my husband and I blanched. Bill was so shaken that, even as the nurses prepared me for surgery, I asked if he was all right. I knew what he was thinking. To us a C-section was bad news, a scar across the belly a scarlet letter signaling failure at the birth game. However, my heart monitor had stopped blipping. I'd had contractions for four days and was more than two weeks overdue. The game was up. Within minutes, I was in surgery.

A knot in Isabelle's umbilical cord later helped explain the erratic heartbeat, making me feel the C-section was necessary—better surgery than a blue baby. Still, I felt some regret about it, and the procedure made my recovery hell.

So I might have been expected to protest when the same doctor scheduled a C-section for my second delivery. The baby was to be over nine pounds, making the risks too great for vaginal birth. And again, I was way overdue. My response this time, however? "Ready when you are!"

Like many women, I'd found my second pregnancy much more exhausting and difficult than my first, largely because this time I'd had to care for a toddler. Pregnant with Isabelle, I'd traveled, taking a last relaxing, romantic trip with my husband to the Smoky Mountains. Reporting a story on coffee growing in Guatemala, I'd gotten star treatment, with people opening doors, carrying luggage, and giving me the front seat in the Land Rover. I'd felt special, excited, and even a little sad to see those magical nine months end. All that anticipation. All that blissful ignorance. Such a great excuse to sleep late. And during that first pregnancy, I actually could.

Research finds that women have more emotional problems carrying their second child than they do their first. No kidding. Here's what I remember of my second pregnancy: chasing, and barely catching up with, Isabelle as she raced toward a major intersection; putting her in preschool and, with my resistance compromised by pregnancy, catching every toddler bug known to man; watching Isabelle fight Bill tooth and nail as he took over the morning routine; and just feeling huge, having gotten pregnant before losing the weight I'd gained carrying Isabelle. I'm sure people would have been nice had I traveled. I don't know. I barely left the house, except to go to the park and the preschool. And in those places, I was hardly a novelty.

I wanted my second child out, and was way beyond setting my heart on a vaginal delivery. If there was one thing I'd learned from my first, it was that the big deal is not the birth, but life with the baby. Soon after Isabelle arrived, I realized that I'd obsessed so much on the delivery that I'd barely planned for the months afterward—to say nothing of the next 18 years.

So when the OB scheduled my second C-section, I felt relieved. No labor! No contractions! No last-minute packing, doubled over the suitcase in pain! This time I had child care to worry about. No frantic midnight calls for baby-sitting! Before, I'd been critical of mothers who scheduled C-sections. Now I felt like I was getting away with something. No juggling contractions with bedtime stories! No counting labor breaths while giving a toddler a time-out! Best of all, I'd avoid the great double whammy of my first delivery: surgery after a long labor. A first-time mom might not get it. The natural childbirth gang will be horrified. But I loved my second C-section.

As a result, I arrived at the hospital calm, my biggest fear—that my whopping nine-pounder would arrive on her own—eliminated. I was so calm, in fact, that when my husband asked to visit his dermatologist in a nearby office for his semiannual cancer screening, I barely blinked. With my first birth, Bill's leaving my bedside for the bathroom had seemed a capital offense. Now going to the doctor as I prepared to go under the knife made perfect sense. One more thing off the burgeoning family to-do list. Go for it!

So off he went, along with the beeper—which sounded repeatedly to summon him from his doctor's office to the birth. He made it, but the dermatologist won't soon forget the visit, which confirmed what I've always suspected: physicians can run on time when they have to.

Jessica arrived squalling like her sister and looking just like her. Mom, however, appeared transformed. In my first pictures with Isabelle, I look like a boxer, smiling victoriously but with deep shadows under my eyes. In the pictures with Jessica, I look so radiant that it's almost possible to imagine that a woman can be prepared for an event as big as childbirth.

Now, it wasn't my fault that I'd been exhausted at my first child's birth. However, I had made a critical mistake *after* Isabelle's arrival that I vowed not to repeat: sprinting at the start of a marathon.

With Isabelle, birth was the big event. I figured I'd dash through the delivery and rest later, when things settled down. My mission at the hospital was clear: deliver the baby and then get a cram course in infant care so I wouldn't kill her. In my free moments, I frantically made rounds of calls to announce her arrival, Isabelle's birth having all the urgency of a breaking news event.

All this made for a busy hospital stay. When I wasn't with my infant or at a baby class, I was on the phone. When not on the phone, I was grilling the nurses about swaddling. When they took Isabelle to the nursery, where she spent her first two nights as I recovered from the C-section, I trailed after, staring at her through the window. And when, on my third and final night in the hospital, they asked if I wanted to "room in" with the baby, I answered with a definitive yes.

"Rooming in." What a cozy-sounding concept. Baby and mother, united at last! And what a perfect way to spend our first night together—under supervised conditions. Evil mommies might condemn their babies to the nursery, but not me.

So the nurses wheeled the clear plastic bassinet into my room, and I gazed at my miracle baby in awe, sleeping with my glasses on so I could scrutinize each breath. For a few hours, she slept. Then she awoke crying at eleven P.M. and stayed up most of the rest of the night. I figured the nurses would fix this little problem and kept pushing the call button. They came. They swaddled. They cooed. They sang Haitian and Jamaican lullabies. And each commented, "What an alert baby!"

Isabelle fell asleep at four A.M. Two hours later, an attendant woke me up to announce that he was replacing all the hospital mattresses; I had to move. He was followed by a nurse taking vital signs, the OB, a photographer selling pictures, an administrator with paperwork, and a man looking vaguely familiar but whom I could no longer identify: my husband.

It was hard to believe that I'd just seen him the previous afternoon. So much had happened since then—an entire overnight cram course in motherhood. Between labor and rooming in, I hadn't slept more than eight hours in a week. "Thank God, we're going home so I can rest," I said as he arrived with the baby carrier.

Ha, ha, ha. With the first baby, the joke is often on Mom. Home, my firstborn continued to defy everything I'd heard about infants. Sleep like a baby? She was up all the time. Newborns don't see well? Isabelle would only stop crying from two to four A.M. if I turned on the florescent lights and gave her a guided tour of the kitchen. By my second child, I realized: they pop out the way they are. Isabelle was highly curious and energetic from birth. While I'd expected to rest at home, she had other plans. A marathon was starting, and with all my early sprinting, I was now out of gas.

Remembering my difficult first weeks with Isabelle, I made several decisions before birthing my second. First, I would not have my toddler visit the hospital. Although the experts say these visits usually go well, I knew that three nights was a short stay (especially compared to the ten days or longer women only a few decades ago routinely were allotted). I wanted to use it all for rest. Isabelle was barely two when Jessica was born. Visiting might be fun, but leaving Mommy was sure to be disastrous.

Second, I left the address book at home. Jessica's birth was exciting, but I now knew that the announcement could wait for anyone whose phone number I hadn't memorized. I did pack five pairs of earplugs, having learned from my first stay how noisy maternity wards can be.

And finally, I decided that no matter how cute my second proved to be—even if she broke all the developmental rules and smiled—I would not room in with her. I felt guilty about this decision. After all, baby number one had gotten the royal, round-the-clock treatment. Yet guilt I could handle. Sleep deprivation after major surgery, I now knew, I could not.

So when the nurses asked where Jessica was to sleep, I was adamant: they should bring her in during the night to breast-feed, then return her to the nursery. "Are you sure?" asked one in a plaintive voice.

"Yes," I said firmly.

"But don't you want to room in?" asked another, giving me the but-what-about-bonding look.

"No," I responded, confident from my superglue relationship with my first that my second and I would hit it off.

Maybe it takes having more than one to hone your survival instincts. With Jessica everything looked so different. The nursery, sterile and cold the first time around, now seemed almost homey, providing something I hadn't noticed before: free, after-hours baby-sitting. Aware of what lay ahead, I was determined to take advantage of it.

And because of this, I enjoyed every minute with my second-born in the hospital. Holding Jessica, I couldn't decide which was more miraculous: her perfectly formed features or the fact that she slept. I'd heard of sleepy babies. Isabelle, however, had convinced me that they didn't really exist. Yet Jessica slept for hours during the day in my arms or in the bassinet by the bed. She slept so much, in fact, that it was as peaceful as being alone.

Alone—in a room with a TV remote, a phone I didn't have to fight for, and food served on a tray every few hours! A friend brought cappuccino. My husband kept the toddler at home. Call me deluded, but I could have sworn I was in a hotel, not a hospital. Okay, one whole night was spent figuring out how to pee. But I got to watch grown-up TV. I had the phone to myself. When my husband visited we talked without interruption. And if my bed didn't vibrate, it did move up and down.

One of my happiest memories of Jessica's birth is of having breakfast in bed while watching TV on Sunday morning as she slept peacefully by my side. A beautiful, healthy baby and room service to boot!

What more could a mom want?

It's hard to predict how a second birth will go. The labor is known to be shorter than it is the first time around, making many deliveries easier. Yet, already stretched, muscles and tissues take longer to heal. Uterine cramping is more severe the second time around. For many women, existing scar tissue makes recovery from a second C-section slower. And as any experienced mother knows, birth often blows out the best-laid plans—even those made with second-time savvy.

Yet if experiences vary, one thing is clear: the *same* woman doesn't go to the hospital twice. And partly because of this, with each baby, a new mom is also born. I think of the woman who arrived for Jessica's birth as slacker mom. It's taken a while to get used to her. I don't always follow her advice. Her standards are so low. She can be so practical and no-nonsense, even selfish and crass, and often leaves me feeling guilty. In the hospital she gave me the distinctly false impression that all first-time mistakes could be corrected the second time around.

I remain forever grateful for her arrival, however. Because while slacker mom doesn't always run the show, as our family has grown, she's the woman who's gotten me through it.

Sex Preferences

I wanted my second child to be a girl.

This wasn't logical. I had a girl already. But having grown up with two brothers, I just couldn't muster any enthusiasm for boys. I like boys—I've liked many way too much, and my brothers are great. I've done the boy thing, though. I spent years watching G.I. Joe get blown up, maimed, and mutilated. I played army and flew toy gliders. One brother's multiple trips to the emergency room for stitches and broken bones convinced me that boys are more accident prone than girls. The other's drum set made it clear that they're louder. I wanted another girl.

So when the technician called with the gender results after a medical screening, I felt like I'd won the lottery a second time. "A girl! And everything looks normal too?! I'm so happy!" I said, bursting into tears.

"Your first girl?" asked the woman brightly.

"No, my second," I proclaimed.

"Oh," she paused, confused. "Well, uhm . . . congratulations!"

The technician didn't get it, but nothing could dampen my enthusiasm. I couldn't wait to tell Bill. Later, after putting Isabelle to bed, I dramatized the announcement.

"The test came out normal," I began.

"Oh, thank God!" responded Bill.

"And, I know the baby's sex," I said coyly.

"You do?" he asked, eyes widening.

"You're not going to believe it!" I said.

"What is it?" he asked.

"It's a girl!" I cried, patting my belly.

Bill leaned against the wall. "You're kidding," he sighed, sinking.

"No. It's a girl!" I said. "Isn't that great!?"

Seeing my husband slump, I suddenly realized that I hadn't thought much about his desires regarding the sex of our second child. Having been through the fertility mill with our first, we had focused more on getting one than on gender preferences. This pregnancy had followed an early miscarriage; our main concern was the fetus's health. Though Bill had said he'd prefer a boy, he hadn't put it strongly and had proven himself the perfect girl dad. Caught up in my own excitement, I hadn't even considered that he might be disappointed.

Yet he looked forlorn. Pulling himself off the wall, Bill said, "Give me a few minutes," and left the room.

Adding a child to the family raises the gender stakes. With just one kid onboard, there's a chance that you'll get that boy or girl that Dad or Mom prefers. When the second or third doesn't help balance the gender scales, however, at least one parent can end up disappointed, especially if, as in our case, the child is to be your last.

In my own family, my grandfather used to call my mother Oscar. Not jokingly. Not occasionally. Always. He'd call and ask, "Is Oscar there?" When my mother and father met him at a crowded bar in New York, he shouted, "Hey, Oscar!" across the room. Growing up, I considered this a humorous term of endearment. Later, I realized that my grandfather had had his heart set on a little Oscar, my mother being his second daughter and last child. My mother took it in stride. "I don't think he knew my name," she laughs today. But I'm glad *I* didn't grow up being called Oscar, Harry, or George.

I was thinking about Oscar and Anne Boleyn, who was beheaded for failing to provide Henry VIII with a son, as Bill walked out of the room. Would my second girl be dubbed little Willie? Would she receive less than a first-class welcome? For many couples, two of the same sex prompts discussion of having a third. I was pretty sure my husband wouldn't want another child: I'd had to lobby for a second. Yet would he love our coming baby less because of her sex? And what about his commitment to the family? It's not just in male-centered countries, such as China, that parents of girls divorce more often than those of boys. The same is true in the United States.

To me, girls had obvious advantages. When Bill returned later, I made my case. Girls, I noted, have fewer problems in school, are less likely to be incarcerated, and care more for their aging parents than do boys. Girls are less likely to break bones and get their teeth knocked out. Having a second girl meant our kids could share a room, clothes, and toys. Think of the savings! The daddy-daughter bond is traditionally the family's sweetest. Finally, Bill isn't into cars or contact sports. Our weekends would be football-free.

My husband, however, wasn't thinking about sports or cars. He wanted a boy to balance the scales, his closest family members—his mother, his sister, Isabelle, and me—all being female. He wanted a boy to help put up the hurricane shutters. He wanted a male skiing buddy, having skied with his own dad, who died when Bill was eighteen.

When my husband mentioned his father, I knew the gender issue ran deep.

"You did say early on that you wanted a boy," Bill noted later, sounding like the victim of a bait-and-switch ploy.

"Excuse me?!" I exclaimed.

"I know. I know," he said, his voice still tinged with betrayal.

As if I could just fix this little chromosome problem. Worried, I turned to him and posed the million-dollar question. "You don't want to have another, do you?"

"No," he answered decisively.

Phew. Little is more difficult for couples than when one partner wants another baby and the other doesn't. "Well, then are you going to be okay with this?"

"Yes," he answered. "But I need some time."

Soon after our gender results came in, our friends Chris and Jonathan got theirs too. Up until now, the couple's lives had paralleled ours. Jonathan and Bill are both law professors who shared a bachelor's pad while waiting for their women to move to Miami. We both married and had daughters a few years later. Chris and I even had the same obstetrician.

Now, over dinner at their house, they announced the big news: they were having a boy. Damn, I thought, watching my husband grimace.

"Wouldn't you know it?" Bill grumbled back home, now envious of both his friend's academic achievements and his future son.

Some matters are definitely better left alone for a while. Saddened by my husband's reaction, but still eager to share my own excitement, I let Bill be and approached our nanny, Nancy. Having worked weekdays for us for several years, Nancy is a special person in our lives. I thought Nancy would want me to have another girl but wasn't sure. Her family in Honduras has so many girls that it's a running joke, and I figured that could cut either way. Still, she loves girls, and I thought she might be excited about another.

"Nancy, do you want to know the sex of the baby?"

"Not yet," she answered quickly.

"Not yet?" I asked.

"Maybe next week. Not now," she said.

Geez.

Getting the cold shoulder at home, I sought out others. My relatives' reaction to the news was positive but subdued: repeat performances aren't a big deal. A taxi driver said I'd need to try for a third to provide my husband with a son. Several grocery baggers, the pharmacist, and the shoe-repair man agreed. A father who shall remain unnamed said I'd never be a "real" parent, and understand the true challenges of raising children, without a son. I considered shipping him Isabelle on a bad day. No one seemed to share my excitement at having a second girl.

At night, Bill dreamed of ski vacations with his dad. I pulled Isabelle's baby clothes out of storage and got weepy over ruffles. A week later, I went back to our nanny.

"Nancy, I'm going to tell you the sex of the baby."

"I'm not ready," she said.

"You're still not ready?"

"No."

"Well, you're going to figure it out soon anyway since I'm starting to get the baby's clothes ready, and I'd rather tell you personally," I explained. "Look, in my hand, I'm holding a plastic heart. If it's blue, it's a boy. If it's pink, it's a girl."

Nancy hovered nervously over my hand. When she saw the pink heart, she clasped it to her chest, burst into tears, and ran out of the room.

Abandoned—again!

Nancy quickly returned and explained that hers were tears of joy and relief. To our nanny, boys were foreign territory. Convinced that I was having a boy, and not sure how she'd handle one, she'd put off hearing the news.

Ah, gender politics. Bill had wanted a boy because he felt surrounded by girls. Nancy wanted a girl, even though she'd grown up with them. At least at the outset, people seem to prefer their own gender.

Yet since then I've learned that while often highly charged, sex preferences are not always predictable, especially in that emotional, last-chance ground beyond one. Everybody at Isabelle's tumbling class thought the couple with two girls wanted their impending third to be a boy. Mom clarified: she wanted a boy. He wanted a girl—and got one. When I offered to give a mother expecting her first son my article on boys and kindergarten, she brushed me away, saying, "No! Don't tell me anything!" Her reaction confused me until later she explained that the prospect of having a boy made her as nervous as a first-time mom. And love, of course, is a great amnesiac. In Robert Stewart's study of couples having a second child, nearly half of the mothers who'd initially wanted a girl could not recall having stated such a preference or even denied having done so once their baby boys arrived.

In our family, gender politics consumed me for a few weeks after the results arrived, then faded. Bill dreamed about his father intensely for a while, then stopped mentioning him. When the baby arrived, I dressed her in T-shirts as often as in ruffles. Slowly, but surely, Ariel, Cinderella, Snow White, and Jasmine became members of the family, and we learned to navigate the hallway without tripping over the dress-up clothes.

There are things, however, to which I will never adjust. I'm still irritated every time the prince rescues the princess in the storybooks. Three females in the port-a-potty on the hiking trail is the pits. I envy Bill's ability to pee alone, his uninterrupted use of his toiletries. If I'd realized that having girls meant years on the pigtail shift, the gender results might have looked different. The firmest equal-parenting agreement is no match for the hair preferences of little women.

I've also learned that girls may not be easier to raise than boys. Different? Definitely. Less active? Maybe, though my oldest now spends almost as much time upside down, doing handstands, as she does right side up, and she climbs door-frames. Yet try—just try—getting girls dressed and out the door. The words on the birthday invitation leap off the page like a bad omen: "Wear your favorite costume. It's a princess party!" Damn. One Ariel outfit. Two who *need* to be her. It's guaranteed misery for Mom. And "nightgowns"—I never even thought about them much before I had two Sleeping Beauties. Now the very word, whispered at eight P.M. by a small princess who needs to change hers yet again, makes my skin crawl. Boys, of course, have their own wardrobe issues, as their mothers often remind me. But as a mom of two young females, I confidently assert: girls' wardrobe fetishes more than make up for boys' antics, and having more than one girl multiplies them.

Still, for the better and the worse, we have become a family of three girls and one boy. Indeed, I got so used to our unbalanced family that I forgot about the gender results until I recently read that many parents are disappointed over the sex of their second child. Delivery-room disappointments are so common, in fact, that some experts advise finding out the sex ahead of time. Recalling his initial reaction to being outnumbered, I asked Bill how the gender issue looked now with the girls three and five years old.

"I'll always feel some loss about not having a boy. Our family isn't balanced. They look to you more as a role model," my husband responded. "The father-son relationship is special. I wonder what it would be like to have a boy, the way I wonder, sometimes, what it would be like to be a doctor. It's a path not taken."

I don't wonder. Having grown up as the older sister to two brothers, I still feel like I know, and despite the potty and pigtail problems, I love having girls. I don't worry about Bill and his daughters because he's never mentioned medical school or called the little one Willie. He's the greatest of girl dads, and I see how much—despite the gender difference—they each take after him. I also don't feel compelled to deliver my husband a son, despite a dozen Miami taxi drivers' opinions to the contrary.

Yet at times I feel for the prince outnumbered by princesses.

And when my husband leaves the toilet seat up, I don't say a word.

Roses in the Bathtub

I would have taken everybody's word for it except for the memory of the roses in the bathtub.

Winter. New York City. New Year's Eve. I'm scrambling to dress for a big evening out with my dark-haired man when a dozen yellow roses arrive from my blond one. The blond is in graduate school in Arizona. Good thing too. Because my New York guy is coming over.

The buzzer to my apartment rings. I throw the roses in the bathtub and pull the shower curtain. Then I answer the door and whisk Tall, Dark, and Handsome to the elevator before he can so much as ask for a glass of water.

It's a festive evening. We party hop. We sip champagne. We do the great New Year's seduction in New York black.

In the morning, when I come home, I find a dozen yellow roses in the bathtub, wilting. A message is on the machine. "Hi Jen. Did you get the flowers? I hope you had a good New Year's Eve."

Ugh—between the champagne and the parties, it had been so easy to forget. I remove the roses from the bathtub, arrange them carefully in a vase, add floral preserver to the water, and put them on the table.

But it doesn't help.

People assured me as Jessica's due date approached that I would love my second child as much as my first. Yet I wondered. In the past, every love interest had come at the cost of another. If a boyfriend came, a boyfriend went. Any overlap between them was at least uncomfortable. Some women can juggle men like bowling pins, barely missing a beat. Maybe it's my Midwestern roots. I'm true blue and loyal, and even little fibs make me feel like a sinner. I got away with my New Year's tryst. Yet those roses in the bathtub made me feel like a no-good two-timer.

So it seemed to me, pregnant with my second child, that trouble loomed. Other women's hearts might expand. Mine, I feared, was of a fixed size and already claimed as far as children went. Even before her birth, my second seemed left behind in the romance department. Pregnant with Isabelle, I'd whispered sweet nothings to my belly as early as four months on. Busy with a toddler during my second pregnancy, I wasn't having those same conversations. Daddy wasn't singing to the womb as much this time either.

Then again, what if I did love her as much, or, God forbid, more than Isabelle? Would my first sense the great betrayal? Would she realize that my heart had been divided? Children may not be like boyfriends, but I wasn't the only one making the analogy. In the classic bestseller *Siblings Without Rivalry*, the description of the older child's feelings upon getting a brother or sister is an oft-repeated one: "Imagine that your spouse puts an arm around you and says, 'Honey, I love you so much, and you're so wonderful that I've decided to have another wife just like you.'" If these were to be Isabelle's feelings, what would be mine? Would I feel as guilty as I had that morning in New York with the roses wilting and the message on the answering machine?

Friends said it would work out fine. Yet they provided no explanation of a phenomenon that seemed to defy both experience and logic. If I were to love Jessica as much as Isabelle, where was all that love hiding now? As my second's due date approached, I felt a little like a traveler of old gazing at the horizon and being told the world is round. How could it be?

So when the nurse handed me the little bundle at the hospital, I observed the moment like a scientist embarking on a great experiment. Was it there? Did I love her as much as my first? More? Not at all?

The answer soon became clear. I loved her as much, but differently. And if I didn't have roses in the bathtub, I did feel a bit like a sneak. Yet cradling Jessica in my arm, I remembered something else: how divine two-timing can be.

Another Tall, Dark, and Handsome—this time in from Paris. We are at the Algonquin Hotel in New York. It's a brief encounter, and for the moment guilt has been suspended. After all, though I still have some hope for Mr. Arizona, our long-distance relationship has only grown rockier since New Year's. Sorting through my overnight bag at the hotel for my satin nightgown, I can't decide which I like better, my lover's accent or the fact that room service has just arrived. I may have felt guilty about the roses in the bathtub, but I'm enjoying the one on the tray.

Now, these were not my feelings in the hospital with Jessica. But weird as it sounds, there were some similarities. No flower—but we did have room service. My first love was out of sight, the idea being, as during that earlier tryst, that if my main squeeze saw me with my new love, there would be a tantrum. As before, I was savoring being with someone whose language I could not entirely understand. And, as before, I was escaping a relationship—this time with a terrible two—that had become so complex that I'd started consulting the guidebooks. With Jessica, as with my Parisian, there were no long conversations about "why" and "why not." Things were simple and clear.

No doubt, being an experienced mother explained some of my lightness. With Isabelle, every early nursing session had seemed so fraught with meaning, so hard. Jessica latched on and that was the end of it. Instead of agonizing about breastfeeding correctly, I stroked her peachy skin. I'd pushed the call button constantly for the nurses' help with Isabelle. With Jessica, I never rang at all. Those smiling moms in the rosy mother-infant ads must all be beyond one; my friends say the third is a charmer, the fourth the frosting on the cake. It's hard to savor love when you feel like you're going to maim the object of your affection: my firstborn had felt so breakable. Holding my second felt as fine as sipping good wine—and this time I wasn't worried about breaking the glass.

So, I enjoyed my first days with Jessica with all the joie de vivre that I had all those years ago at the Algonquin. Only one small, sneaking thought bothered me, as it had then. How, later, would I reconcile my feelings with those for my first love?

Back home soon after, the little red light blinks on the machine. Putting Jessica on my shoulder, I play the messages. "Hey, Jen, I heard you had another baby! I'm sure she's as beautiful as the first one. Congratulations! Call me when you get a chance . . ."

Now, it's been hard to keep track of Mr. Arizona all this time. Since graduate school he's lived a lot of places, done a lot of things. Somehow, though, he always finds me. After Arizona he moved to New York and we spent some time together. Yet it wasn't meant to be; he went his way and I went mine. Today, he's married. But we remain good friends.

It takes time to realize how flexible and enduring love is. From having two brothers, as well as a father and stepfather, I long ago learned that love isn't limited. Yet even knowing this, in those first weeks after Jessica's birth, I still worried that it might be. For I continued to love my daughters so differently. I loved Isabelle with all the passion of a two-year relationship. We'd scaled the heights. We'd survived the depths. We were bonded with superglue. After Jessica's birth, I realized that nothing could dampen my passion for my firstborn. I might run out of time. But I'd never run out of love.

And Jessica? For a while I loved her simply because she slept—my gratitude after Isabelle's nocturnal antics was so profound. I loved her with the serenity of an experienced hand. I loved her with the fierce protection that comes for a newborn and your youngest child—and in that way I clung to her harder, responded to her more than to Isabelle. I appreciated her in a way you can only appreciate the baby who is your last.

Back home, these feelings at first came into conflict. At times the baby felt like an intruder, disrupting my heretofore-exclusive relationship with her sister. On other occasions, Isabelle's toddler antics drove me crazy; I just wanted to be alone with my infant. Early on, I continued my affair with my second clandestinely, pretending to be nursing behind closed doors while Bill handled Isabelle, but really tickling Jessica's toes. Sometimes I felt guilty about this. For there was no denying it—as an experienced mother, I was enjoying baby number two far more than I had baby number one.

It took a while to get over feeling like a two-timer, to realize that I didn't have to hide my love for my second daughter from my first, to feel confident that the heart does not divide, but expands.

However, when Isabelle asked if I loved Jessica more than her, I knew what to say: "I love you because you are Isabelle. I love Jessica because she is Jessica."

Surprisingly, this explanation has sufficed.

But then, all these years later, Mr. Arizona leaves messages on the machine. And I always return his call.

Sibling Rivalry

I am an expert on sibling rivalry and have the credentials to prove it. First is a battle scar: a chip on my lower front tooth that I got when my brother Jon, at age four, threw a magnet at me. Second, living proof on Amazon.com that this same brother —three years younger than me, no less—went into my chosen profession, proving to be both talented and prolific. And finally, my own humble literary beginnings: a full page of rhyming lyrics written at age seven with the refrain "I hate Jon."

Growing up, I experienced both the limitations and frustrations of being a big sister, even as my nemesis proved a great playmate. If Jon hadn't wandered off at the New York Automobile Show, we might have seen more of the city and less of Dad's apartment that weekend. If he hadn't dumped his crayons out on East Eighty-seventh Street, we might have had more interesting outings. When he dug up my dead turtle, whom I'd buried under a cross of sticks, I ran away to the woods behind our house, only returning later because I missed my mother.

In our family, sibling rivalry seemed a given. My mother raised me on such vivid stories of being taunted by her older sister that for years I thought "birdbrain" was a swear word. My aunt and mother's relationship came around, and Jon and I are now close. Yet as my due date approached, I alternated between feeling like a traitor to my firstborn and fearing for the life of my second.

I also wondered whether Isabelle would be a good big sister. Except for making Jon eat dog doo, I, of course, had been the perfect sibling—patient, loving, and kind. Isabelle, at two, showed none of these qualities and was so attached to me that Bill practically had to tie her down to brush her teeth. How would she share Mommy's affection with another small person? And even if I were to love both of them equally, how could I possibly provide enough attention for each?

In the long run, I was sure a sibling would be a great gift, Jon, with time, having more than made up for his early offenses. Over the years, I've also grown closer to my other brother, Steve, despite a fourteen-year age difference.*

But in the short run, I braced myself for big trouble.

To prepare, I started reading, beginning with Vicki Lansky's *Welcoming Your Second Baby*. Lansky addressed one of my concerns right off the bat, advising that a preschooler be told about an impending sibling two to three months before the arrival. Yet along with such helpful pointers, she added a lot to my to-do list.

* *Because of our age gap, Steve and I didn't spend many years growing up together. Thus he's spared here. He's also my half-brother and has a different father than I do, so he does not appear in a later chapter on siblings concerning my Dad.*

The list of possible activities to ease my first child's transition seemed endless. I was to "borrow" a baby or baby-sit one "regularly" to get my first child used to infants, or better yet, expose her to various infants so that ours might look like one she'd seen. I was to take Isabelle to my OB appointments and consider enrolling her in sibling classes. Before going to the hospital, I could bake a "birthday" cake with her to freeze for a baby party later. Another suggestion: tape bedtime stories for my firstborn to play in my absence. ("And don't forget to say good night at the end of each.") Back home, I was to get Isabelle a pet ("if you can handle it"). And finally, presumably feeling sprightly after the OB appointments, party, and pet, after the baby was born, I was to stagger the children's naps to spend time alone with my first child.

Maybe it was the early fertility work. After years scheming to get pregnant the first time around, I found it hard to feel anything but joyous over conceiving a second and just couldn't muster such a guilt-ridden reaction. These and similar suggestions in other books seemed especially ridiculous given my unwieldy state. Dad was barely mentioned (though Lansky suggested I "let" him spend time with the older child while I nursed the baby). Following some of Lansky's advice, a friend had taken her child out of day care to see our chronically late OB and ended up with a screaming toddler in the waiting room. Every mom in the park said the name of the game was to synchronize naps.

The sibling sections of the toddler books had better advice. Giving the firstborn big-kid privileges later proved critical. Having Isabelle help me bathe Jessica was messy but worthwhile, showing me early on how much big sister wanted to help. Acting conspiratorial with the first toward the second ("Can you believe the baby did that!") also smoothed relations, and didn't involve any class fees or baking. But overall, reading these books while pregnant confirmed my sense of impending doom, each citing parent after parent who'd expected sibling harmony and instead ended up with a slugfest.

All roads led to *Siblings Without Rivalry* by Adele Faber and Elaine Mazlish. Their suggestions made perfect sense to a sister with a chipped tooth and a prolific brother. I didn't need the book to tell me not to compare my kids. With my battle scar and broken Barbies, however, it was news that I shouldn't referee all their fights, frequent parental intervention having been found to escalate rivalry. Later, stepping back allowed them to resolve some of their disputes themselves and relieved me from playing cop when it wasn't necessary. The prescription to provide for your kids according to their individual needs rather than equally is also wise and would have saved me from buying the baby sunglasses if I'd followed it. No doubt, *Siblings Without Rivalry* is worth a read and can even save you money.

Yet the book's popularity left me pessimistic. *Siblings Without Rivalry* was a monster bestseller when it came out in 1987 and has been in print ever since. A few years ago, the authors published an expanded edition. If so many parents need help with sibling relations, weren't we doomed? What had I been thinking when I'd conceived a second partly to provide our first with a sibling?

Discouraged but determined to prepare, I turned next to the children's books on siblings, picking up *Angelina's Baby Sister.* In the book, Angelina has a full-blown tantrum, kicking her dresser and hurling toys across her room after her family ignores her when baby sister comes home. It's a beautifully illustrated book, with a good plot and real action in the destroy-the-room scene. However, while Isabelle was in the midst of the terrible twos, she hadn't yet attacked her dresser. Why give her any ideas?

Disturbed, I mentioned my concern about sibling strife to our Latin nanny. Nancy looked confused. Though she'd heard a lot about sibling rivalry, the idea didn't resonate much. "Why do you Americans talk so much about sibling rivalry?" she asked. "In Honduras, we think siblings are great. I'm excited for Isabelle."

Nancy's comments made me wonder. Could my fear of sibling rivalry be a cultural phenomenon, my American sense of individualism fueling a fear that my kids would clash and compete? I wasn't sure, but as I watched our nanny in the weeks that followed, one thing became clear: while I'd been preparing my daughter for trauma, Nancy had been preparing her for joy. Her approach wasn't entirely kosher. The experts said not to present the sibling as a gift, and Nancy acted like Christmas was coming. Yet her attitude resonated a lot more with my own sense of excitement than did the experts' decidedly negative messages. And, best of all, it didn't add anything to my to-do list.

So as Jessica's birth approached, I put the books away and took a position: two is great, even if one of them doesn't get it at any particular time.

The experts say the siblings' first meeting isn't crucial. However, like most mothers, I scrambled to do it right, focusing attention on my first, not my second, as the two met at our house. Yet when Isabelle demanded to hold Jessica, all I could think was, *Here it comes—the bop-the-baby-on-the-head scene.* The sibling horror stories were so ingrained, I didn't even think to hand Bill the camera. So I missed it: the picture of my two year old in pigtails, all smiles as she tenderly held her newborn sister.

Every photographer remembers the pictures he misses more than the ones he captures.

Nursing was the next great hurdle, and, as in all sibling matters, I'd heard horror stories: mothers whose first went bonkers whenever the second breast-fed, women who'd stopped nursing due to interference from another child, and, at best, exhausting acrobatics by Mom to amuse the toddler while feeding the baby. From the stories, it sounded like nursing was best done on the sly, and so, initially, I tried to sneak off with the baby. This worked when Bill or Nancy could distract Isabelle. Quickly, though, I realized it wasn't a strategy. Babies, after all, nurse every few hours. Anyway, what was I trying to hide?

So, cringing at first, I nursed Jessica with Isabelle at my side, letting my toddler investigate the entire affair. She stroked the baby's head. She loved tapping her finger on the breast pump's air hole. Sometimes she got disruptive and I got mad: it's hard to feed a hungry newborn with a toddler interfering. Other times, though, she put her baby doll to her own chest and we nursed in tandem. Occasionally, I could even read her a short book while nursing.

Then something happened that I'd never expected or read about: Isabelle got bored with my breast-feeding. Jessica's arrival sparked significant toddler sleep disruption. The night I paced at three A.M. with the baby and stumbled into Bill in the dark hall carrying our toddler remains vivid. But though she sometimes tried to pull me away from Jessica, Isabelle generally didn't fight me over nursing, realizing, perhaps, that it wasn't negotiable.

Still, I continued to look for sibling rivalry and was sure I'd found it one evening when Isabelle threw a huge tantrum as I tended Jessica, then two months old. However, my firstborn's mood improved so drastically upon eating crackers that it must have been low blood sugar.

I figured sibling rivalry would raise its ugly head once our younger child crawled. Yet Isabelle was so amused by her sister's one-kneed approach that this went well. I looked for sibling rivalry as Jessica began to walk, but the bigger threat proved to be big sister's efforts to get little sister to dance. Finally, I figured sibling rivalry would strike with full force when "mine" became our younger daughter's favorite word. And at this point Jessica had developed a nasty pinching habit. Given her normally sweet temperament, this surprised me until I read that the second is usually more aggressive than the first. Isabelle retaliated. Screaming and crying ensued. Yet, while intense and furious, the fights passed quickly.

My children are now three and five. They can go to the mat over a barrette. Doors slam. Claims are made. Birthdays are difficult. The day big sister got the blond Barbie and little sister got nothing is one I remember well. Yet sibling rivalry, on the scale that I'd expected it?

I've looked everywhere but under the couch, and it just isn't here.

Several factors may explain this relatively harmonious state of affairs. My own early experience undoubtedly sensitized me to sibling issues. The first rule of parenting more than one is to avoid comparisons. I would no more compare my kids than lock them in the closet. When a father in the bookstore said angrily to his toddler son, "Why can't you sit quietly like your big sister during story time? I'm so proud of her," the hairs on my arm stood on end. You can win in this house, but only in your age category, currently nursery school and kindergarten.

My stories of Uncle Jon's early shenanigans probably help validate some of Isabelle's darker feelings toward Jessica. If the chipped tooth is a battle scar, it's also a handy souvenir, a reminder that despite some bumps and bruises, things often turn out okay. Every dentist gets a gleam in his eye when he sees it, and every one is rebuffed.

More important, probably, is the fact that between Mommy, Daddy, and Nancy, my kids have multiple caretakers and don't have to compete for the attention of one strung-out mom. Research shows that the older child adjusts better when the father is actively involved with her after the birth of a sibling. Presumably other caretakers, such as a babysitter or a grandparent, make a difference too. Help has allowed me to carve out time alone with my firstborn, which all the experts agree is critical. Frankly, I can't imagine anything worse for sibling relations than two or more little ones competing for the attention of one exhausted caregiver 24/7, whoever it may be.

Then again, who knows why siblings get along? My decision to integrate Isabelle into Jessica's life early proved right on: most experts now dispute the notion that brothers and sisters should be kept separate and the baby fed apart. Yet putting Isabelle in preschool a few months before Jessica's birth so she'd have some sister-free time once baby arrived also seemed to ease our firstborn's transition, increased colds notwithstanding. Parents serve as models: maybe Jessica and Isabelle get along well because I don't fight with my husband in front of them. It could be chemistry, or because mine are both girls—though the barrette battles challenge this theory and studies find girls more jealous than boys. Perhaps it's because they share a room. Or maybe it's in spite of this.

Possibly sibling stories are like birth tales—you remember the bad ones, making strife seem more common than it actually is. The story of the girl who pulled out all her fingernails after her sister was born certainly proved a lot more memorable than my friends' reports of brotherly love. Cain and Abel endure. Yet despite such tales, research increasingly finds that rivalry is only part of the sibling story. "More important," notes Joan Solomon Weiss in *Your Second Child*, "is the bond of love and loyalty that develops between most brothers and sisters and that deepens with the passing years."

Likely, Isabelle is just a better big sister than I ever was. She's definitely nicer than was my husband, who pushed his younger sister down when she was learning to stand. Jessica is a lot sweeter than was toddler Jon. So much is also a matter of perspective. Having gone to the mat with my brother during his wrestling years, my kids' fights seem pretty tame. Parents without siblings are disturbed by brawls that appear normal to me.

It also could all change tomorrow. Isabelle has not yet learned to write or gotten her adult teeth—the possibility of battle scars and nasty songs remains. And if I don't have sibling rivalry, I do have a playdate problem, one sister always being left out when the other has a friend over.

In any case, for the moment, I'm savoring sibling harmony, on all fronts.

And this could be a problem. For if I don't stop gabbing with Jon on the phone and emailing him about the day's events, I'm never going to finish writing this book.

Great Expectations

You could not step twice into the same river;
for other waters are ever flowing on to you.

—HERACLITUS,
GREEK PHILOSOPHER
(540 B.C.–480 B.C.)

And so, for enlightenment, I take you back to a conversation that preceded our second child's birth. . . .

Ten days and counting until Jessica's due date. Lying in bed, I begin the great pillow adjustment process, trying to find some way to get comfortable and sleep with my bulging belly. "I am so ready to have this baby," I groan, feeling like a beached whale.

"Can't you keep her in there a little longer?" says Bill, looking up from his book. "It's a lot easier now than it will be later."

"Easier for whom?" I shoot back, thinking of bopping him with a pillow. Then I notice how glum my husband looks, and irritation changes to concern. "What's the matter? Aren't you excited about having the baby?"

"Sure," he says, looking as excited as a condemned man. "It'll be great, in the long run."

"In the long run?" I ask, female hormones suddenly flaring in that volatile, age-old mix of fear of male abandonment and anger that he, who has no chance of experiencing a contraction, has any worries at all.

"Well, it's going to be difficult for a while," Bill asserts gravely. "Isabelle didn't sleep well that first year, and she still gets up sometimes. How are we going to handle two at night? And remember that battle at nine weeks to get Isabelle to take the expressed milk so I could feed her? I know it was hard, but you weren't exactly easy to live with during those first weeks. I also worry about how having a second is going to affect us."

Does he have to remind me? I married my husband partly to gain access to his massive brain and near-photographic recall, my own memory being highly selective. Though he can't find anything in the refrigerator, Bill remembers the details of *Ulysses*, which he last read in college. But the closer we get to Jessica's arrival, the more this amazing biocomputer is proving a mixed blessing. For in addition to remembering the sweet moments with our firstborn, Bill has perfect recall of a lot of events a pregnant woman would rather forget.

He's also got plenty of material. Our first year with Isabelle was trial by fire. Unlike many couples, we had no help and no local relatives to pitch in. Bill knew nothing about babies. I knew little more. While he'd agreed to share parenting, my husband had no domestic skills. I wanted him to anticipate my needs, but I had not mastered telepathy. Fraying nerves further, our first was an active baby and lousy sleeper—

so bright-eyed, in fact, that when a friend once mentioned her infant's steady sleep patterns, I almost burst out crying. It was Bill's announcement during Isabelle's first week that he was going to take a nap that provoked me to throw the pot at him. I never threw anything else, but the verbal volleys to establish shared parenting lasted about a year.

Yet it's precisely because of those difficult days that I'm able to comfort him regarding his main concern, our marriage. The fact that we survived and created workable family roles convinces me that we can handle a second. Any woman who gets a square parenting deal from a man who is all thumbs in the kitchen soon forgets the trials and tribulations and lives in eternal gratitude—especially given how many fathers opt out. For over two years, I've bragged about Bill to any mom who will listen, and some have used his example as ammunition in their own marital negotiations. Surely it's easier to be the pot thrower than its target, but, as I point out to him, our relationship is reason for confidence.

The experts advise getting help with the second child. I note further that this time, unlike early on with Isabelle, we'll have it. Like most wives, I'm an excellent armchair psychologist. With a little coaxing, Bill comes around. Soon after, he's snoring by my side.

I try not to wake him as I adjust the pillows again. I'm still uncomfortable, however, and Bill's fears have reignited some of my own. For having had one perfect, healthy baby, it seems too much to ask the universe for two. A little voice haunts me: why didn't you quit while you were ahead? Since my first, I've heard so many more stories, seen so much. How can I possibly expect another miracle?

Then again, what if she is as bouncing and bright-eyed as Isabelle? My memory may be spotty, but some scenes are indelible: up every hour for weeks with the amazingly alert baby on "vacation" in Colorado; hysterical from sleep deprivation visiting Washington, our hotel room so fascinating to baby at two A.M.; dark thoughts deep in the night back in Miami, imagining throwing little Miss Bright Eyes out the window. The very idea of more sleep deprivation sends my mind reeling. How will I survive it with two?

I may have been starry-eyed and ill prepared during my first pregnancy. Yet ignorance is bliss. Tossing and turning in bed, I miss those rose-colored days. Though experience surely helps, right now it's not consoling.

So I adjust my pillows and roll to one side, then to the other, until, determined to savor the last of my peaceful nighttime hours, I finally drift off too.

"You're kidding!" exclaims Bill, shaking his head as he arrives at the hospital two days after Jessica's birth.

"Don't worry. She's fine. Maybe it's just your timing. She did open her eyes a few hours ago, and they're beautiful. But every time you visit she's asleep." I pause before daring to make the assertion. "She seems to be a sleepy baby."

"A sleepy baby?" My husband shakes his head. "I can't believe it."

The first sign that things were going to be different the second time around came in the hospital: unlike her sister, baby Jessica loved to sleep. She slept in my room. She nursed with her eyes closed. She greeted my husband with a hearty roar at birth and then slept through all four of his visits to the hospital. He didn't see her awake until he came to take us home.

Our other concerns were quickly alleviated as well. It had taken ten minutes of teeth gritting and tears to get out of the car after my first C-section. After the second, I opened the car door and emerged with barely a wince—probably because, unlike with the first, I hadn't gone through labor. We'd planned to have help the second time around. But we hadn't realized how much easier life with a baby is with an extra set of loving, competent adult hands. No wonder my friend whose mom had visited after her first baby's arrival had looked so tranquil! Bill's handling Isabelle in the mornings allowed me to recover from nighttime feedings. Nancy's help during the day allowed me to nap. As a result, I wasn't nearly as sleep deprived with the second as I'd been with the first.

Then there was the miracle in the kitchen. One night, as I nursed baby Jessica, I looked up and saw my husband cooking veggie burgers. He'd never cooked them before. In the past, I'd gotten dinner and he'd cleaned up. And I hadn't even provided my usual elaborate instructions for such tasks. He'd just seen that I was nursing the baby and started dinner. For a man who'd barely been able to boil water when we met, this was a great leap forward.

With our first baby, I'd launched a feminist revolution in our own house. Now Bill was cooking veggie burgers: the world had changed. All those fights on "date night" during Isabelle's first two years were paying off. Many men wait for the second child to become involved fathers, so they have a lot of catching up to do. And few, of course, ever really share the load. But by the time Jessica was born, Bill had two years of intense childcare behind him. We'd already hammered out most of our major parenting agreements: he did house maintenance, I did kids' clothes, holidays, gifts, and minutia; we took the children for roughly equal amounts of time and divided the dishes. A thousand tiny agreements defined our days. As a result, just weeks into life with two, we found ourselves on a comfortable, if hectic, autopilot. The battles had been fought, the big ones resolved, useful routines established, and some unrealistic expectations—a hot, homemade meal on the table every night at six—abandoned. I didn't have to be the bitch in the house anymore.

Soon after Jessica's birth, the man who'd looked so glum before her arrival turned to me in bed chipper. "You seem okay," he said, smiling.

Okay? Are you kidding? I felt blessed. My biggest fear—about the baby's health—was history. Our infant was not only thriving but sleeping. My husband had stepped up to the plate, and though we didn't have any family nearby—still a major disadvantage—Nancy filled the gap. And big sister hadn't even asked to send little sister back to the hospital. Knowing that we didn't want another child, the phrase "getting your body back" had even begun to ring with possibility.

A few weeks after Jessica's birth, I was on a new baby high.

Then our infant started to cry.

Now, as an experienced mom, I was used to babies crying. I'd played the crying game with Isabelle in cars, airplanes, restaurants, and hotels. I'd listened to friends' babies scream through entire playgroups, and watched scores of children wail at the playground. I'd even learned to write—not brilliantly, not happily, but word by painful word—listening to a tantrum outside my door.

However, Jessica's cry at two weeks was unlike anything I'd ever heard. It was incredibly loud. If you didn't hear it, I'm surprised. And it was relentless—neither diaper changes, rocking, singing, swaying, nor swaddling soothed her. Coming from a newborn, it proved particularly heart wrenching. Hour upon hour my tiny baby wailed nonstop, tiny chest heaving, fists clenched, face contorted—and there was nothing we could do.

At first I thought Jessica was dying. When she didn't die, and just kept crying, I figured it was my milk. When she kept sucking, growing, and crying, I decided she had a severe personality disorder that would put her on the street, penniless, years later. The wee hours are perfect for replaying the family mental illnesses. After doing some research, Bill said it was colic.

Colic? My baby with colic? My sweet sleeper now shrieking nonstop every night? This seemed impossible. Isabelle had never had colic. I'd never had colic. Colic wasn't my thing, just as picky eaters aren't my fate. Though I'd had friends whose babies had had colic, I knew nothing about it, having skipped colic in the parenting manuals to read about sleep problems.

But the baby gods love to throw curve balls, and a new child gives them a whole new set of pitching opportunities. From my growing a family, I've since learned that if the birth goes easily, you'll get mastitis. If breast-feeding is a cinch, the baby will get colic. If colic doesn't strike, teething will be a nightmare. And if all passes smoothly, stay mum. No other parent wants to hear.

I had to have colic. I was due.

Yet because I hadn't experienced it, Jessica's colic threw me. Sleep deprivation felt familiar, the enemy I understood. Colic was new and scary. Though I felt like an old hand caring for the baby by day, as I paced and rocked our screaming infant at two A.M., I felt as incompetent as a first-timer. I knew the colic would end. Isabelle's tougher phases were history. Yet how would my precious little one ever turn out normal given such a fitful start?

I was at the end of my rope when my friend Jen gave me the mom-to-mom colic talk. Bill doesn't understand why a mother's words carry more weight than his research. But there aren't any well-adjusted toddlers who had colic pictured in the books. Jen's daughter, who had had terrible colic, was now thriving. My friend assured me that Jessica would be fine and that the whole thing would probably pass when she reached three months—and she had the toddler to prove it.

As my baby screamed each night, I held on to her words with all the fervor of a first-time mom.

Jen was right. At exactly three months, the colic passed. After weeks of midnight coddling, jostling, singing, and multiple movie rentals, the screaming stopped. Jessica had already started smiling during the day. Now she bloomed. Blond hair replaced the brown she'd been born with, her blue eyes sparkled, and except for some dog-eared pages in the child-care manuals, not a trace was left of this difficult time.

Colic was one example. Looking back a few years later, I can see that there were many others. As experienced parents, we had a lot of great expectations regarding our second child. Yet few panned out, proving that old adage that worrying wastes time because the things you fear rarely occur, while others you never expected do. Instead of a year of sleep deprivation, I got three months of colic. Fearing intense sibling rivalry, I later faced the challenge of siblings in cahoots, "C'mon, Jessica, let's hide" becoming my older child's response to bedtime. Everybody said the second child would be easier. Nobody provided the critical qualifier: only when you're handling one at a time. What proved my greatest challenge—getting baby, toddler, and gear around town—was something I'd never even contemplated during my pregnancy. And I doubt that even my husband recalls the first time Jessica drank the expressed milk, she slurped it up so fast.

Bill's expectations also failed to pan out. Braced for marital strife, my husband found himself instead in a solid, if rarely serene, partnership, a doubling of the opposition forces quickly consolidating the adult camp. We had other problems—like having a conversation. But it's hard to accuse your spouse of slacking off when you are each scrambling after a small child. With two, we were clearly on the same team, even if, at times, the inmates seemed to be running the asylum. While women rightfully become resentful when husbands fail to do their part with two kids, when you do share it can lead to an even greater sense of equality than the first time around.

All of this has led me to conclude that while it's great to be an experienced mom, a little knowledge can be dangerous. We all tend to project a future that looks like the past. The more you know, the more you think you know what to expect.

Yet with children, as in life, there are no real repeat performances. Family life, like a river, keeps changing. Every child, like every moment, is new.

But I'll leave it to my husband, with his prodigious memory, to remind me of this, as well as of the exact day that the screaming stopped and the smiling girl emerged.

Lonely in a Crowd

"How do you do *free time?"* she asks, as we rock our newborns.

Now there is a strange question—an intelligent woman asking how I "do" something neither of us has. She hasn't asked whether I *have* free time, though this is the real issue. She also hasn't asked what I *do* with my free time, sensing that this is presumptuous.

"What free time?" I respond.

"Yeah, I feel good if I can just shave my legs in the shower," she says, visibly relaxing.

I've been here before. Do I want to have this conversation again? Andrea is the sister of my friend Pam, who invited us for dinner because we both have new babies. But this is her first child and my second. Aside from a certain shared level of sleep deprivation, we live in different worlds. A novice, she's eager to do things right and seeks my advice. However, since I'm a second-timer, my standards have fallen: I'm the one licking the dropped pacifier and putting it back in baby's mouth. And some things I've learned, I'd rather not share.

At dinner, Andrea moves her stroller closer to the table, afraid that a passerby will steal her newborn. This seems absurd. Then I remember my experience as the frightened new mom with the breakable baby just two years earlier. I had nightmares about Isabelle's survival. And I recall sharing our bed with the baby—it had sounded so sweet. However, after trying it just once, I awoke every night for months after to search the bed, certain my husband had squished our infant, even though she dozed peacefully in the nearby bassinet.

Yet I've slept with baby Jessica often. It helps that Bill now sleeps in another room, but I'm also not so worried about Jessica's survival. Indeed, the entire sleep debate now seems overwrought. What's the big deal? You either sleep with the baby or you don't—whichever works.

But my new friend doesn't ask about sleep. She asks about travel. Dare I describe the "vacation" my husband and I took in Colorado when Isabelle was five months old? Some nights she woke me up every hour. Was it altitude? Travel adjustments? We never did figure it out, though we spent much of our vacation reading about baby sleep. I've solved the travel problem with our second baby largely by staying home.

I can't tell this to a new mom, though. She's bought her plane tickets and wants encouragement. She thinks I've got it together. So I change the subject to one that new parents love: gear. As a second-time mother, I've grown skeptical of equipment. My garage is full of baby stuff that proved useful anywhere from an hour to three weeks. One device did make a difference, though: the baby sling. The sling has been our great equalizer. I feed the baby. Bill carries her. Maybe the sling can save this woman's marriage too.

I show my new acquaintance how to adjust the sling. She smiles politely, then demonstrates two additional sling positions that she learned at a La Leche League meeting. Leave it to a first-timer to have the latest moves. I may have wisdom, but she has all the newest information.

Andrea is great—nice, fun, smart as can be.

But we're not going to be baby buddies.

With my first child my social life boomed—any woman with an infant was fodder for friendship. It was like the time I lived in Nicaragua, when sharing third-world conditions made other expatriates instant allies. I met Andrea's sister Pam two years ago at the café where we are now dining. After a brief conversation—"You're home too? This is *so* new for me. . . . Is yours sleeping?"—we met regularly for several months. When three women in my writers group had their first babies, a playgroup sprang up as naturally as grass in a meadow.

Since Jessica's birth, however, I've become surprisingly isolated. The first-timers' talk of teething bores me to tears. My mantra—that having two makes one look easy—isn't what they need to hear. I've made too many changes since Isabelle's birth to relate to that great, vaulting leap first-timers are making from one life to another. Stopping in at a church playgroup with Jessica, I hear it: "Desitin or A and D Ointment?" "Crib or bed?" Like most Mommy-and-me gatherings, this one consists mostly of new mothers. After fifteen minutes, I flee.

My needs are now also different than those of my friends who stopped with one. When, as new mothers, we used to meet in the playgroup, Sara and I always had great conversations. I was looking forward to something similar when she invited me to come by after Jessica was born. "It's a pool party. Just bring the girls over," said my friend. Eager to see her, I did. Yet she had only one to watch by the water. I had a toddler and a baby; Bill was out of town. By the end, I was happy just to get my kids home alive. If Sara and I talked, I don't remember it.

The women I have the most in common with—other mothers with two or more—are beyond reach. Conflicting nap schedules and busier adult lives often make it impossible to get together. At the park, our children pull us in different directions. After constant dashes to the swings and slide, I finally give up on talking. When, another time, I do focus on the conversation, an earsplitting scream sounds from high atop the monkey bars, and I turn to find Jessica dangling precariously by one arm.

And the moms working outside the house with more than one child? Surely it's easier to get an appointment with the president. When not at the office, these women want to be with their kids. I don't take the cancellations personally. At some point, though, I stop trying.

Yet life without friends is like dinner without dessert. What to do?

It takes persistence to get three of us mothers, each with two kids, out to dinner one night. But there, finally, we sit, the wine soothing, the fish delicately spiced, listening to Bach, not Barney. Then it starts: the school conversation.

Public versus private. Class size. Waiting lists. Deadlines. Good teachers. Bad teachers. Aftercare. Redistricting.

I've launched these discussions myself. The more kids you have, the more important these talks. Having discussed preschools all week with my husband, though, I need a break.

"Can we talk about something else?" I finally ask.

"Yes, please. Let's do!" says one of the women.

"Sure," says the other, sipping her wine. Then, after pausing for a moment, she asks, "What are you doing for summer camp?"

It's Friday night, about a month later. Bill is caring for the kids while I dine with friends. None of them has children. None are married. They can't talk preschool and don't get the pajama routine.

It's great.

Some say you can't expect to relate to friends without children once you become a parent. But the fact that these friends can't understand my life makes them my salvation. With two kids, I've been in the game long enough to forget how weird it is. Let's face it: talking to other moms is comforting but not always a reality check.

However, my childless, or child-free, friends say wonderful things like "Gee, you definitely deserve one night a week off," or "Wow, I don't know how you do it. I took my niece and nephew out the other day and it was a nightmare. You need three adults just to take two kids to the beach." And "Well, if I ever married again I would have separate bedrooms. I wouldn't want to share *my* space."

When they pull that "poor burdened mom" business, I point to their litter boxes and vet appointments. Unlike most of them, I'm pet-free. I may change diapers, but I don't sport a pooper-scooper. Kids, of course, are a lot more demanding than cats or dogs. Yet pets give us common ground. We've even had pet-kid playdates.

My friends are a lot better with my children than I am with their animals, though. Free of daily parenting responsibilities, they muster amazing energy to play when they visit. Jeannie gives my girls first-class belly-dancing lessons. Joann's roughhousing with Isabelle and Jessica is exhausting just to watch. As a mom, I have to pace myself with the girls or I'd be dead by ten A.M. Yet if my friends make me seem boring, I'm always glad for the entertainment.

Best of all, my single girlfriends are available for adult evenings like tonight's gathering. Over sushi, we talk—about dinner parties, to which I'm no longer invited, news I haven't read, clothing stores I haven't had time to visit. They tell hilarious date stories, and I try to recall: did I ever meet a hunk in the grocery store? They'll never understand how I can live with a man who is so messy. And I save my bad-mommy-day stories for my parent chums, who know that their backdrop is joy, not sorrow. However, the question that dinner with my childless friends raises is an important one that rarely comes up on the mommy evenings.

Who are you, how are you, without kids?

With my first child, I needed a baby buddy.

With my second, I want a girls' night out.

Sweet Silence

It wasn't until I had my second child that I realized what makes babies so special.

They can't talk.

This revelation was influenced considerably by the fact that Isabelle was two when her little sister was born. Anyone with a two year old appreciates a respite from words. It's exhausting to answer questions all day about how the world works, tedious to negotiate simple matters like putting on shoes.

After taking my toddler to the grocery store for a particularly large run over the holidays, I was ready for an isolation tank. "Capers?" asked Isabelle. "What are capers? Why a big jar? Why not a small jar? Can I open it? Why not?" Multiply this conversation by $150 worth of items, and Mommy returns home a jabbering idiot.

I don't remember my first daughter's silences as a baby. I remember wanting her to talk. I thought language would be such a great leap forward. With words we would bond more, discuss things, have conversations. She would say she loved me, and understand when I said I loved her.

I didn't realize that for an entire year her favorite word would be "no."

But in my baby's silences, I always imagine her saying "yes." We watch television, I tickle her toes, and I know she feels the same way I do about the recent election. I open the door in the morning, she smiles, and we agree that it's a beautiful day. In silence, my baby and I reach complete consensus. I have a constant audience, an absolute confidant, the perfect keeper of secrets. And unlike other people in my life, my wordless wonder never tires of what I say.

My infant is also the only person to whom I don't have to talk. There are no questions to answer, no explanations to give, no verbal demands to respond to ("I want the red one, not the green one!"). Unlike the FedEx man, she doesn't expect me to say, "Hi, how are you?" and comment about the weather. I don't have to be civil at all.

On days when the phone won't stop ringing and the fax keeps beeping, I retire to my bedroom with my baby like a desert traveler to an oasis. I haven't enjoyed a wordless relationship so much since "Big-Eared" Steve shot me those long glances across the room in fifth grade. (One of many such romances that peaked with silence and died with words.)

Of course I often break the silence. I tell my baby about my day. I make weird noises. I have long, one-way conversations.

Yet it's a different kind of talking than I do with anyone else. With my baby I can converse with abandon. I can start songs and get the words wrong or not finish them at all. I can switch thoughts midsentence. I can be illogical. My baby is the only person in the world with whom I don't have to make sense.

My little one's silence liberates everyone around her. Confronted by a person who cannot take orders or discuss the

Dow, the hard-boiled businessman begins cooing. The shy lady behind the deli breaks into song. Silence encourages quiet people to speak up and loudmouths to turn the volume down, as day-to-day personalities and agendas are set aside in an effort to elicit one small smile from her quiet countenance.

Language will soon transform both my baby and the world around her. Adults will begin to feel compelled to explain things in rational ways, and the more she talks, the more my daughter will demand such explanations herself. With words, her personality will begin to surface, like sculpture emerging from a lump of clay.

I look forward to that. However, I'll also miss the mystery and possibility of her silences. I'll miss imagining that she is smiling at me because of her great love rather than because she wants to pull the barrette out of my hair. I'll miss the sixteen possible personalities I projected onto her, even as I delight in the one that speaks up. With language, a world will be gained. Yet a more quiet, peaceful one will be lost.

Children don't seem to fully acquire their identities until they talk: notice how people refer to "the baby," but call a toddler or older child by name.

With words my baby will become known as Jessica. She'll start grabbing for the phone. She'll ask for candy in the checkout line. It will be nice, on occasion, to know just what she wants. But other times it will be tedious.

And then, I'll count on the romance that started in silence to carry us through.

Errand Girl

As I arrive for the preschool pickup, Isabelle runs and jumps into my arms. "Mommy, Mommy, where are we going?!" she asks excitedly.

Well, let's see. Florida is a Mecca of major children's attractions. Within forty minutes of Isabelle's school are Seaquarium, Metrozoo, and Parrot Jungle, to name but a few. If we hightail it, we can make it to Disney World by dusk.

Hmm. "You want to go somewhere special with Mommy?" I ask.

"Please! Please!" Isabelle begs, tugging on my dress.

"Okay," I answer. "Shall we go and push the green button?"

"Yes! Yes!" my firstborn jumps up and down again then runs to her teacher, shouting, "I'm going to push the green button! I can make copies all by myself!" Then she dashes around the playground as I gather her lunch box and artwork.

Kinko's, here we come.

After Jessica's birth, I faced two problems. First, with a new baby onboard, one of my worst fears about having another child—neglecting my firstborn—was coming true. Though I tried to make time for her, Isabelle was getting far less attention from me than she had before. Busy with Jessica, I often brushed my older child away. I'd gained one daughter, but my big girl was suddenly Daddy's charge. Once my precious little one, Isabelle suddenly seemed at times like a huge, boisterous menace—a feeling that had started when she tried to jump on me toward the end of my pregnancy. Intent on protecting the baby from my toddler's dangerous, if well-meaning, antics, I barked orders and reprimanded her more than in the past. When, sensing my harsher attitude, she whined, I felt both irritated and guilty, worried that I'd caused her behavior.

At the same time, a growing family required more errands. If we weren't out of diapers or wipes, I needed food for the preschool party. Busy having babies, I'd put off many domestic projects for years. The front hall closet was jammed; finding things in it was impossible. A pile of ripped dresses for mending lay on my closet floor. Shoes needed to be resoled, laces replaced. Yet finding time for errands was difficult. Trying to do them with a baby and toddler on Saturdays proved exhausting. Bill took the kids and our one car on Sunday, leaving me gloriously free, but without wheels. And I wasn't paying for childcare during the week to go to Walgreens.

So as things settled down after the arrival of our new addition, I started doing errands with Isabelle after school while Nancy watched Jessica. This went badly at first. The drugstore is a drag with a two year old, the toy aisle one big booby trap. If you shop for something as fun and climbable as furniture, leaving is traumatic. During Isabelle's twos, errand time also coincided with the post-preschool slump.

Then my older girl turned three, started napping less and later, and got in the car in five minutes rather than ten. Instead of staging protests, she wanted to help. At Kinko's, she pushed the green button and copied my phone bills. At the ATM machine, she punched "make deposit" with glee. The ripped dresses on the closet floor got mended, shoes were suddenly repaired. We so enjoyed revamping the front hall closet with stuff from the Container Store that we returned three times. "Hello, Isabelle. Hello, Jennifer," the salesman hailed us on our third visit.

Now, I wasn't surprised that Isabelle loved the copy store and drycleaners. As an advocate for simplicity in an overly commercial parenting world, I believe that toddlers can be just as entertained at the car wash as at Disney World, and for a lot less money. One of the delights of little kids is their appreciation of small pleasures, their perception of the mundane as miraculous.

What surprised me was my reaction when a girlfriend with two young children said she felt guilty about schlepping her older on errands on Saturdays, while Dad watched the baby. "Why?" I asked, surprised. "Errands are fun!"

Errands are fun? Riding the escalator at Target thrilling?

Who is this woman shaking her booty to the music at Kinko's while copying her hand?

Years ago, when Bill and I were deciding whether to have kids, I wrote an angry poem about motherhood called "Driving." A badly written diatribe, the piece reflected my concern that motherhood would turn me into an unappreciated errand girl and domestic drone.

Now, there's no doubt that parenting chores get tedious. If I'd known how often my lunches after I had children would be a tuna fish sandwich eaten at stoplights, my poem would have been a lot longer.

But as we leave the preschool, it's a clear and breezy day. I've got my three year old all to myself. Isabelle is bright-eyed, bushy tailed, and ready for action. Ah, what joy to venture out with someone you don't have to carry! No stroller to unload! No diapers and wipes to schlepp! There's nothing as easy as one civilized three year old when you're used to managing two wiggle worms. The poet of the past could not have understood. Yet perhaps you can only appreciate liberation after being firmly tied down.

Hand in hand, mother and daughter embark, the world—rather the mall—our oyster. At the shoe repair store, Isabelle finds a stray lace and claims it like a treasure. "How cute," coos the man behind the counter. At the drycleaner's, we watch the seamstress stitch a hem. "*¡Que preciosa!*" smiles the lady sewing. We stop in the market's restroom but sneer at the diaper-changing table. "We don't need that today!" says Isabelle.

"No. Jessica is too young for errands," I remark gravely, watching my big girl's face light up.

At Kinko's, we make fifteen copies of my latest magazine article, four of Isabelle's hand, and two of mine. At the bank drive-thru we deposit checks, watching as the tube sucks them up and magically delivers them to the teller. Take that, Magic Kingdom! Touché, Toys"R"Us!

I hate to say it. It's so uncool. But seeing the world through my firstborn's eyes, the bank drive-thru looks amazing to me too.

Back home, Isabelle greets baby Jessica with a hug. Maybe it's a justification for leaving my second child behind. Yet I'm convinced that the errand hour has made Isabelle a better sibling, having watched my firstborn deteriorate into a pile of mommy need when we don't get out together.

Not that Kinko's or even the Container Store can make up for all of our losses. Every time I hear the mother of an only child talk about her kid's sophisticated books and fabulous outings, those losses hit home. If it weren't for the little sister who eats sand, my big girl would be going to the beach every weekend. And if I weren't reading to Jessica at the same time, Isabelle would be listening to more advanced stories.

Yet having a sibling more than compensates for most of those losses. And if Isabelle and I are no longer as close, a little breathing room may be a good thing too, given the separation that lies ahead.

My relationship with my firstborn is not the same as it was before her sister's arrival. However, something essential has been preserved at the copy store and pharmacy, our mundane missions making for a little island of mommy-daughter intimacy in a family now structured around the needs of its youngest.

Before Jessica was born, people advised me to let others tend my infant so I could spend time with my other child, arguing that while the baby wouldn't know any better, Isabelle was used to my attention and would need it. This, at the time, struck me as terribly unfair. What about the little one's rights and all that mommy-baby bonding business I'd heard so much about the first time around?

Now I think it's excellent advice. A baby's velvety skin and tiny wail will always claim a mother. When you're trying to nurse a newborn, an older child's well-refined whine is irksome, her vocal demands a drag.

It is important to do something special with your firstborn as the family grows. But by doing errands I've learned that you don't have to do anything fancy or expensive. You just have to do it together.

Isabelle is no longer my one and only. Instead, she's my errand girl. And driving has never been so much fun.

Second Place

In a large, windowless room in a Miami hospital, I sit on the floor in a circle with twelve mothers and their babies. At the front, a nurse holds a dummy infant and provides a demonstration, her words punctuated by tiny wails. The mothers have the dazed, starry-eyed look of first-timers. One wants to know about baby gas. Another asks about pacifiers. Gently, the instructor returns the discussion to the task at hand: infant massage. Bottom sore from the floor, I think, massage—oh yes! Wouldn't that be nice!

I tried hard early on to be a first-time mom to my second child. Instead, I became a class dropout: the baby activities that had seemed so important with Isabelle were now tedious. I quit infant massage after one session, my butt too sore to return. I abandoned the local Mommy-and-me group, ears ringing, after fifteen minutes. For a while I took Jessica to a tumbling class. Then writing called, and I quit that too.

Across the board, my younger child seemed to be getting short shrift. Unwilling to have any baby-sitter for Isabelle during her first months, I sent my second baby into Nancy's strong arms for hours a day. While her sister's scrapbook bulged, Jessica's birth pictures sat in their envelopes. Isabelle had a strawberry Napoleon cake and fifteen people at her first birthday party. Jessica had Duncan Hines cupcakes and one friend. "*This* is Jessica's party?" asked the friend's mom, surprised to learn that she was the only guest.

I'd expected Isabelle, not Jessica, to take the back seat as our family grew. The parenting guides, after all, dwell almost exclusively on the tender feelings of firstborns, and especially early on, I was consumed with the baby. However, eventually I managed to carve out some time alone with my firstborn, the errand hour, in particular, keeping us firmly bonded. We weren't as close as before, but by her third birthday, Isabelle was also becoming more independent and didn't need me as much anyway.

Yet what about my baby? For Jessica wasn't just getting less of me than Isabelle had: the quality of my attention was also different. While I'd encouraged my firstborn's growth, buying developmentally appropriate mobiles and toys, with my second I was a slow-track mom, savoring her stages, in no rush to move on. By the time Jessica arrived, I'd woken Isabelle up so many times tripping over the talking alphabet board that I'd given it away. Once I'd seen how quickly my first had developed playing with kitchen pans, the squawking "learning" toys looked ridiculous. The pediatrician assured me that lack of such stimulation wasn't the reason Jessica was taking longer than Isabelle had to talk. With a little spokesperson, second kids often have less need to speak. Still, I wondered: was I stunting my little one's growth?

As time passed, my persistent, gnawing guilt concerned my younger child. I loved both girls. Yet Isabelle had gotten the lion's share of early pampering. With my second, in contrast, I sometimes even appeared coldhearted. Bill and I debated sleep strategies for a month before we let Isabelle cry it out. With Jessica, I just plugged my ears and closed the door. More relaxed and experienced, I enjoyed Jessica's early days more than I had Isabelle's. But compared to the first time around, I seemed to be missing some essential mommy-baby experience. Maybe, I thought, this was because Jessica and I weren't in a playgroup. Maybe we weren't spending enough time together. Or maybe I was just a bad mom.

Because from all appearances, Jessica was in second place.

Lunchtime. I've just picked up Isabelle at preschool. Nancy is returning from an outing with Jessica, who is eighteen months old. I hear the little footsteps in the foyer and go to greet Jessica. Crouching, I wait, arms outstretched, mommy heart aflutter. Almost nothing is better for a mother than greeting her kids.

This time, however, the joke is on me. Shouting, "Boo! Boo!"—her best pronunciation of Isabelle—my little one toddles right past me toward her big sister. Today Mommy, not Jessica, is in second place.

Guilt is one thing. Falling off the pedestal is another. By the time she ran past me, Jessica and I were bonded. I didn't doubt her love. And she didn't seem to doubt mine, which, if not initially as intense as it had been with Isabelle, grew to equal it. I also knew that, despite diminished attention and sparse scrapbooks, second children generally do fine.

But our relationship was very different than mine with Isabelle. My first had favored me so much that she'd put my husband and me at odds. ("Having a few problems in your marriage?" laughed an expert I interviewed for an article on toddler favoritism.) Jessica also usually turned to me first. Yet other times I competed for attention with her father, her sister, Nancy, her blanket, and her thumb. If Isabelle's love was laser-like, focusing on Mommy, Jessica's was more diffuse, lighting up everyone around her.

This was great for the family. Two girls who favored Mom might have trashed shared parenting for good. Finally, Bill was getting his due. When Isabelle gave Daddy the cold shoulder after he returned from a business trip, Jessica's hearty welcome made up for it. And I was glad my little one loved her sister. Having a sibling more than compensated for anything I failed to give her. After serving as Isabelle's human pacifier, it was also a relief to have some breathing room.

Jessica thrived, smiling early, sleeping well, and eating with gusto, the classic easy second child. Her sunny disposition seemed living proof of the experts' assertion that less attention can be a good thing.

Yet, after years as Mother Superior, playing second fiddle has proved an adjustment for me. It's humbling to see one's best antics outmatched by a preschooler, startling—when you've been the comfort object—to be passed up for a dirty yellow blankie. Isabelle's early developments were all mine. Jessica took some of her first steps with Nancy, and her first swim strokes with my landlubber husband. With Isabelle, I fought for equal parenting, pried her little hands off me to leave the house. With my second, I've been jealous and had to learn to share.

And at times I've thought, what does this easy-second-baby business say about Mom? For as my children have grown, it's become clear: the kid in whom I invested less is more easy-going than the one who got more. On difficult Isabelle days, I even wonder if I'm a bad influence. Did I ruin my first? Is her temper my fault?

On a hot Miami afternoon, Isabelle is climbing the kitchen cabinets. Jessica sits smiling on her father's lap listening to him read.

I'm eating humble pie, pondering my demotion.

Less attention may be a good thing, but it's going to take some getting used to.

At the Oasis

Shhh. Don't tell. Don't say a word. I'm in our bedroom in the back of the house with the baby, the door shut tight. My husband thinks I'm nursing and is preparing our two year old for school. So please don't tell him. At the moment he won't appreciate the news: that his wife is really on vacation.

Much has been made of the benefits of breast-feeding. But it's only with my second baby that I've discovered one of its key advantages for Mom: nursing can provide a break.

Imagine, after these years spent chasing a toddler, lying in bed! Watching grown-up TV! Drifting off, with a gorgeous, velvety-skinned companion who doesn't demand that I read aloud! Outside the bedroom door, pandemonium reigns. "No!" screams Isabelle. "Time-out!" yells Bill. Inside, I run my fingers through hair as silky as down. On the *Today Show*, parenting expert Vicki Iovine is about to discuss getting your groove back as a mom. No way am I opening that door now.

With my first child, nursing was a mountain to be climbed. The learning curve was steep, training sessions sleep deprived, and I felt as natural as a human turned cow. Behind my awkwardness lay the fear of failing motherhood's first great test. Was Isabelle latching on properly? Which pump was best? How fast should it work? Were my nipples supposed to be sore? Was the baby eating enough? How do you nurse around strangers?

With Jessica I am both experienced and beyond viewing breast-feeding as a competency test. I want to nurse my baby, but having seen kids thrive on formula, I'm no longer on a crusade. A purist with my first, I now supplement the breast with the bottle, guilt-free.

Breast-feeding now appears as just one of many parenting issues, almost insignificant compared to the challenge of getting a toddler ready for school. To bare or not to bare is no longer a question, my nursing identity now firmly established. I'm a breast-feeder who likes a little coverage, and having worked hard to integrate baby number one into my adult life, I've got the nursing wardrobe to provide it. Whether I'll use it, now that I barely leave the house, is another matter.

With Isabelle, I sometimes nursed every hour. Fear of infant dehydration? Only a first-time mom could explain. With Jessica, I'm happy to share my breasts but ready, too, to reassert my claim. When I'm done, I'm done. No marathon nursing stretches this time.

Finally, I'm also beyond the great nursing fallacy: that breast-feeding "sucks the fat off you." How we new moms waited in Isabelle's baby group for this fabulous phenomenon to occur! However, the only mother who slimmed down quickly was the one who bottle-fed. Breast-feeding made the rest of us ravenous *and* big. From this and other unscientific data, I've developed a theory: skinny women lose weight nursing. Women who love food get fatter. But the good news is that since we big eaters never skip meals, we don't run out of milk.

So now, instead of feeling guilty about being a glutton, I'm enjoying the ride. And what a ride it is! Seconds on potatoes, large portions, the perfect excuse to seek refuge at toddler birthday parties and put your feet up at home. Nursing in the glider when Isabelle's at school, I can even read a book. And it's not *Winnie-the-Pooh.*

However, it took a few months for me to realize the critical benefit to Mom of breast-feeding the second time around. You see, as I noted earlier, Isabelle is pretty good about my nursing Jessica. Yet is there any need to tell Bill that I can breast-feed around her? After some initial forays, I abandoned nursing on the sly, feeling that Isabelle should get used to it. Lately, though, I've begun doing it again—this time because of its advantages for Mom. Nursing the first time around put so much of the child care on me. Now, with two kids to manage, it's the great equalizer.

You see, a man will never question breast-feeding. The whole thing mystifies him and makes him feel slightly useless. He can't tell if the baby is nursing or asleep. He doesn't know that by your second you could nurse standing on your head in a crowded bus. If you say, soberly, "I've just got to get some peace to nurse the baby. She hasn't eaten for four hours," and head for the bedroom, only a real heel will let the toddler follow.

So it isn't fair. It's rare. Yet it's true: this morning I've got the better end of the stick. Like I said, though, please don't tell my husband. Consider, as I do, that despite the shrieks, major daddy-daughter bonding may be occurring outside my door. She isn't enjoying my absence. Neither is he. They both want Mommy to themselves, breasts and all.

However, nature calls. This time self-nurture too. And if I get my groove back, who knows what could happen?

The Sex Police

I will not think of having sex in the kitchen.

That is, I will not think of having sex while cleaning up and watching my husband eat Shredded Wheat out of the box with his hands. I will proceed with my plan.

It's Monday night. Isabelle, who is two, has crashed, exhausted after a preschool party. Jessica, now six months old, is in her crib. The kitchen is cleaned. The lunch box is packed. I've put a candle in the bedroom, fetched matches from the high shelf. Though my black bra is tighter than it used to be, it has a certain uplifting effect.

This could be the night! I tiptoe toward the bedroom.

"Mommy?" Isabelle stands in a stained Cinderella nightgown rubbing her eyes.

Busted. Again.

Bill and I used to have a nice little adult sex life. Even after the first baby, we managed to make that great milestone—sex at six weeks. Our desire for a second, aided by Isabelle's naps, kept the flame alive. We even managed amazing feats like having sex in the evening.

Two small children, however, have doubled the obstacles to nuptial bliss. First, there's the large leap from the preschool discussion to lust. Then there's the germ factor—the best-laid plans dashed when Romeo reaches not for me, but for a Kleenex. Finally, there are the little sex police next door. Having two small kids is a double prophylactic. If one doesn't get you, the other one will.

Lately, I feel like an adolescent again—sneaking around, constantly being interrupted, admiring a guy from afar but not getting anywhere with him. Not since high school has so much planning gone into doing so little or have the obstacles to romance been so formidable.

I thought things were bad at seventeen when I discovered that my brother and his friend were spying on me and my boyfriend through the den window. Jessica has a sixth sense for sabotage, crying the moment the bedroom candle is lit. Isabelle recently found my diaphragm. I said it was a plug, to be used only by Mommy for big leaks. This satisfied her. But I'll probably find it in the sink next.

My attitude has also become juvenile. Forget the joy of sex. I'm back to the achievement of sex. I'm trying, once again, to get away with something. And just like those early days, lust is mixed with a little loathing. Let's face it, when you don't do something often, you lose confidence. Can a married woman forget how to do it? It's hard to believe, but true: I got further in my parents' den when I was in high school than I often do in my own bedroom now.

When the obstetrician pronounced me fit for fooling around six weeks after Isabelle's birth, I took his words as a prescription.

When he said the same thing six weeks after Jessica's birth, I laughed. With one child we were a couple with a baby, romance still part of the marital equation. Now, with double the kiddie load, we're platonic partners, or shift workers. Lately we've been setting marital records for abstinence, sex now in competition with the one thing we really can't get enough of: sleep. If it's "use it or lose it," Bill and I are in for trouble.

Thus it's fear—of the deep freeze's becoming permanent—as much as lust that has me digging through my lingerie drawer. The experts say parents' sex lives take a bigger hit after the second baby than after the first. Yet until reading Vicki Iovine's *The Girlfriends' Guide to Getting Your Groove Back*, I'd figured our little problem was temporary. However, Iovine, who with four kids should know, devotes an entire chapter to reviving the flagging sex lives of parents whose children are old enough to dress themselves and swim without floaties.

So I'm following Iovine's prescription not to plan sex while cleaning the kitchen, her words "It always sounds like a bad idea when you're looking at a sink full of dirty dishes" having hit home. This groovy mom's admonition, on the *Today Show*, that you will enjoy it if you just start, echoes in my ear along with her reminder that sex keeps women young and attractive. My husband's comment about missing "romance" also pushes me on, a wife's guilt as motivating at times as her own lust.

Persistence! Perseverance! Nothing as complicated as sex ever happened between the parents of two little ones without some conniving.

I got away with a lot in high school.

Can't I get it on as an adult?

Thursday night. We're going to put the kids to bed early. Bill has heard this before. Four stories. Three trips for water. Everything hinges on Isabelle, who's been popping up after we put her down. Will she or won't she?

Dishes, floor, and lunch box done, we tiptoe to the bedroom. Before we would have primed the stereo. Forget it. Our atmospherics are down to one candle now. It's hard to find the matches. But I persist, our one prop essential to Dad's transformation to seductive mystery mate—research showing that men's doing housework turns women on notwithstanding. Lighting the candle, I listen for the *rap-rap* of that little knuckle on the door.

Instead I hear . . .

WHAAA! Jessica. Nightmare? Dirty diaper? By the time I figure it out, it's past our bedtime. Call it a curfew, and it's an earlier one than I had at seventeen. I won't be grounded if I stay up past ten, but I'll feel that way.

Foiled once more!

Lately I feel like I'm living with my parents again. If my mother went upstairs when my high-school boyfriend and I went to watch a movie in the den, my stepfather would often head us off in the kitchen, peppering my basketball player with questions about his game.

Now, if it's not Isabelle, it's Jessica.

Sunday night. The experts say couples with young children should have sex—to keep the bond alive and calm nerves frayed by missing sippy cups and toddler tantrums. But I don't care anymore. As in adolescence, when I spent hours hunting for nonexistent parties, I'm tired of the chase. And that's good. Because at nine, with the girls finally asleep, my husband calls the hurricane-shutter man.

In Miami, where we live, hurricanes are serious business. This dicey subject has put the kibosh on many an evening, as my husband has explained from his side of the bed how the shutter men never show up and I've portrayed from mine a horrific scene of flying kiddies and shattered glass.

I figure it's going to be a long call. We have lots of windows. That's okay, though, right? Any mom knows that survival is more important than sex. Anyway, tonight I've made other plans. *Simple Abundance* sits on my bedside table. If I can't live clutter free, I can at least fantasize about it. Who needs physical contact, anyway? Between my toddler and baby, I've been groped and fondled all day.

I'm deep into simplicity and sachets when my husband enters. The shutter man is coming tomorrow. I've heard this before.

This time, though, my man no longer looks like a fellow with shutters on his mind. He looks, instead, like that basketball player did when my parents left town.

"It's nine-thirty," he whispers, smiling.

I am not in the mood. My nightgown is shaped like a tent. The black bra is in the laundry. And it feels strange to kiss someone with whom I've barely spoken—just as it felt odd in high school to ride home from a party with a guy I barely knew.

Yet we both know an opportunity when we see one. And opportunity, these days, is what sex is all about.

I close my eyes, letting my clutter-busting scheme go.

The planets align. Mystery man is mine. And on this rare night, I feel like I did in the back seat of the car on that moonlit street the police forgot to patrol: almost, for a moment, like a real adult.

Muscles and Wrapping Paper

It's a hot, humid Sunday morning. I watch, nervously, as my husband straps a crying newborn and wiggly two year old into the car. Will the expressed milk run out? Will Jessica cry during Bill's silent Quaker meeting? I can't imagine how this will work. For I've yet to take them out alone myself.

Bill and I hammered out our fifty-fifty parenting arrangement with Isabelle—the flying pot the first salvo in a yearlong battle to put policy into practice. Yet, while we finally arrived at an equitable distribution of labor, with Isabelle, I was the leader. I gave the first bath. I served the first solids. I demonstrated how to grind peas to a perfect pulp. Bill eventually became sleep chief, getting our firstborn when she woke up at night. But mostly, we let maternal instincts guide us.

Now my husband is venturing out alone first with both the kids, and I'm watching from the window. Seeing them leave, I feel conflicted—grateful, yet displaced, and also worried that the outing will be a disaster. Infant and toddler at Daddy's silent Quaker meeting? Give me a break. I can barely handle them in the living room.

So I'm prepared for the worst when my clan returns a few hours later. However, Bill's smile, while frayed around the edges, spells victory. All has gone well. Jessica even drank the milk. And I detect a bit of macho bravado when he swings the baby carrier into the house.

One Sunday leads to two. Soon Bill is taking them every Sunday and some Saturday mornings too, allowing me to recover from the long night shift with Jessica. Each time my man returns he proudly counts the hours he's been out like a runner training for a marathon. First it's three. Then it's four. On a hot steamy Fourth of July, he takes them for five—to the same playground that recently left me sandy, steaming, and sweating after just two. "For five hours!?" exclaims a fellow mom whose husband is far from setting any child-care records. "What did they do?"

The traditional wisdom is that the first baby makes a family and the second makes a father. Research shows that men spend more time doing domestic chores and childcare after a second child arrives. In cases where they don't, but could, mothers often become resentful, stressed, and exhausted: it's one thing to make dinner with a baby on your hip, another to do it caring for a baby and a toddler while dad is watching TV. "I think the second child was so hard because this time I expected him to help and he didn't," explains one friend. As the portraits of the couples in *The Second Shift* make clear, marriages often suffer dramatically when men fail to share the domestic load after the birth of a second child. The experts agree: the new arrival necessitates Dad's stepping up to the plate.

But from my experience, this advice gives fathers far too modest a role. For if one child demands parenting skills, two or more are an exercise in brute strength. Any man who's willing to flex his muscles can clearly not only step up to the plate, but lead the game. The same kids who had me soaking my feet each night were light free weights to my husband. I finally got it one day while watching the short fellow at the gym lift twice as many pounds as I, at five foot eight inches, can. Men are better designed than women for parenting a clan.

It's not just muscles that give fathers an advantage. In addition, men have a keen sense of self-preservation that women sometimes lack. The maternal instincts that served me so well with one torture me with two. As much as I want to, I can't respond to both when they cry at the same time. Bill can read a book while they holler—a fact that undoubtedly helps explain his long outings.

I hated my husband for this insensitivity with our first child. I still sometimes hate him for it now. Yet lately I also find myself observing him with a new fascination.

As Bill slings the baby carrier into the car like some swashbuckling rodeo champ every Sunday, I start to wonder: is he on to something?

Fall. Isabelle is three, and her preschool is raising money by selling wrapping paper. The form and catalog are a fifteen-minute project—exactly my amount of time for the exercise bike. "What do you think I should do with this?" I ask, showing Bill the wrapping-paper form.

"Throw it away," he responds, after scanning the paper quickly.

"Throw it away?" I ask, incredulous. "It's to raise money for her school."

"Well, fine, if we need wrapping paper, order some."

"We don't need any. I just got a bunch on sale at Walgreens."

"Then just throw it away," sighs my husband.

But of course. There's not a man in Miami who has filled out the wrapping-paper form. Men know how to deal with the trivia of parenting. When a mom at the preschool parents' group complained about her toddler's hair-brushing traumas, Bill offered a male perspective. "Cut the hair!" he advised, getting attention, if not agreement, from Goldilocks's mom.

With our first child, I wanted my husband to do more. In the biggest fight of our marriage, I raged about all the tiny chores I was doing, of which he was unaware. We had a fifty-fifty parenting deal, but the small stuff—and it's almost all small stuff—gravitated to me. It took almost a year to figure out how to divide duties and continued effort to keep things equitable.

These days, we still occasionally fight about details, and a list of who does what goes up on the fridge. Yet in many ways the parenting equation has changed. For even after we divide things up, there's still too much to do. If before I got angry because my husband was reading instead of putting away toys, I now more often look up to see a man cleaning up Play-Doh. I can't just ask Bill to do more. Like me, he's doing all he can. I have to do less.

So, with guilt, but conviction, I pitch the wrapping-paper form. Soon after, I start to draw other lines, trying to cut the

Gordian knot that is now family life. My target: the little tasks that keep moms frantically busy but that men manage to ignore. The first call is easy: toddler birthday presents.

Ah, how I have heard the complaint, and made it myself. "When Bobby is invited to a birthday party, my husband thinks he's really 'working' by dropping him off.... But he doesn't think of what I did: shop for the gift, buy a card and wrapping paper, wrap the gift, look for tape, look for ribbon..." laments one mom in *Twice Blessed*, a book on having a second child. Is this our battle cry, "Equal time at Toys"R"Us!"? Instead of complaining, let's cut the crap. No one should do some of these errands.

With my first child, I forgot that birthdays are an annual affair. Getting to Isabelle's first was such an accomplishment that I was eager to celebrate. I was also happy to buy gifts for her little playgroup friends, who, all firstborns themselves, actually needed them. By Jessica's arrival, however, Isabelle and her friends had accumulated far too much stuff, and I'd discovered the buying power of grandparents. Shopping for a gift, barely manageable with one toddler, is suicidal with two. Buying presents for an older child, who can actually connect the present with its giver, makes sense. But a gift for the toddler who has everything?

So I tried to simplify gift giving. Initially this did not go well. Following a man's example is one thing, feeling good about it another. Unlike Bill, I felt like a heel arriving empty-handed at the birthday party. When I rewrapped a present we had received and my friend exclaimed, "Oh, Jennifer, you shouldn't have!" I felt deceptive. When the toy truck I bought at the supermarket—one of the few places I shop alone—broke on first use, I felt like a cheapskate, especially since the recipient's mother was a thoughtful gift giver. No wonder so many preach but so few practice simplicity. It often makes you look like an idiot.

Declaring that Isabelle's birthday would be a no-present party proved equally problematic. Everyone brought gifts anyway, except for one friend, who'd bought a gift but left it at home after getting my message not to bring a present. Making matters worse, her daughter became hysterical, fearful that hers would be a no-gift party too. Isabelle was fine with the policy, but I felt ridiculous.

I've read of a recent trend toward no-gift parties. Hmmm. From what I see, people may be interested in changing the rules of the game, but they're not cutting back. Consider one mom's question to Miss Manners in *Child* magazine, regarding her three year old's birthday: "Is it rude to note on the invitation that an option for a present could be a check payable to my daughter's college fund . . . ? My children have generous grandparents who give them enough clothes and toys throughout the year. I don't want to be rude to my guests, but I believe money toward the college fund would be more useful than things the kids don't really need."

Miss Manners put this parent in her place, noting that "The proper response to having a surplus is to give to the needy, not to plead the need for something more." Yet questions like these have made me realize that a no-gifts policy probably isn't going to work.

And so, finally, I have struck the right balance, buying gift certificates from our local bookstore. Presto! With one fell swoop I support our independent bookseller and solve the birthday problem. By putting the mom's name on the certificate I give the gift to the person who really deserves it: the exhausted hostess.

"Gee, maybe I'll use it for myself," smiled one mom recently upon receiving the certificate.

Please do!

Attempts to follow my husband's lead in other areas have gone more smoothly. Until kindergarten, Isabelle had short hair, saving us years of brushing trauma. With a little convincing, our daughters have come to believe that small Christmas trees are the cutest. Last Thanksgiving, we skipped that great eating orgy that traditionally opens the female cooking season, packing turkey sandwiches for a picnic instead. People forget how little it takes to please small children. Delighted with the sandwiches, Jessica serenaded us all afternoon with her preschool turkey song.

Keeping things simple has had one major unexpected advantage: my kids have reasonable expectations. For her sixth birthday, Isabelle is going to a movie with a friend and then coming home for cake with a couple others. Having never seen a movie in a theater before, she thinks this is big stuff. No bounce house. No costly clown. No tracking down moms for RSVPs and sending out thank-you notes. And all for the price of a few tickets to *Peter Pan*.

Not that I always follow my husband's lead. Like all moms, I have my sacred cows—little things I enjoy doing and won't abandon. Bill cringes when I get out the kids' crafts box. Glitter, glue, pumpkin seeds, lentils, feathers—it's an unholy mess, of my making. One mom's simplicity is also another's deprivation; if you like to buy gifts, the fancy wrapping paper will probably please you. Some of my friends cook so well that it would seem criminal if they didn't share their talents. And, of course, men can be great gift givers and cooks too.

Meanwhile, if I need to lower my standards, Bill could definitely raise his. When I had to cut bubblegum out of Isabelle's hair after he let her pick it up off the sidewalk, I felt like bagging equal parenting for good. ("But when I was little, I picked up cigarettes and put them in my mouth," he explained, as if that made it better.)

Generally though, since Jessica's birth, I've tried to follow a new standard: if a father won't do it, and I don't enjoy it or find it important, I won't either.

In the details department, I've decided to mother like a man.

It's a year later. Jessica is two. Isabelle is four. I'm spending the afternoon with some mom friends.

"Jennifer has her husband well trained," one smiles slyly.

I start to protest, then stop. This makes Bill sound like a lap dog rather than a partner. And yet I did train my husband that first year with Isabelle. I had to. He had no domestic skills and knew less than I did about babies. Like anyone else, myself included, he would have avoided the dirty work if possible. You can teach a man competence, or you can teach him incompetence. As *Halving It All* makes clear, to get a square parenting deal, women often have to demand it.

"Training" my husband has no doubt made our life easier with two. What I could never have predicted, however, that my friend's observation misses, is that Bill is now teaching me a thing or two. Because of our setup, it didn't take two kids to make my husband a father. It did, however, take two to make shared parenting truly equal. It's only now that I realize that fifty-fifty means being a follower as well as a leader.

Yet before I can explain, the moms want to know: how does our arrangement work? I start by noting that Bill and I trade off mornings getting the kids ready. Hearing this, one mother bursts into tears.

This woman works full-time. Her husband, who works too, won't even wash a dish. The house, the children, and everything that goes with them are her responsibility. The other women gathered are worried about how stress is affecting her health.

"Oh, but he's a great father," she protests, her eyes ringed red with exhaustion.

A great father?!

I have heard this before: he's a great father, but not a good husband. Being a great father usually means something like playing with the kids. Not being a good husband means acting like a big child. In the end, the childcare load a mom bears is determined by the maturity of the man in the house.

Now, I could tell this woman to mother like a man, but she'd think I was crazy. I could suggest that she ask her husband to father like a man; however, she thinks he's doing that already. And it's difficult to imagine this mom passing on the wrapping-paper campaign, or arriving empty-handed at the birthday party.

So I offer my condolences. What can I say?

Real men are hard to find, motherhood almost impossible to simplify.

And wrapped in the right paper, a cage can look like a gift.

Creature of Habit

By the time the baby was six months old, I had recovered some semblance of equilibrium. It was six more months, though, before I felt able to go out of the house with both children without another adult to help.

—Rebecca Abrams,
Three Shoes, One Sock & No Hairbrush: Everything You Need to Know about Having Your Second Child

It sounds so great—a beach outing with the kids and my friend Jen and her baby and toddler! A sun-filled, fun-filled mommy day! If Bill can venture out with them, then so can I. And now that Jessica is sleeping better, I've raised my sights. Weekdays we stick close to home. However, Saturdays we're going to do special mommy outings. We'll go to the zoo, attend art festivals, and visit Seaquarium. We'll do something different every week. Saturday is going to be fun day.

So I'm feeling chipper, even singing to Barney, as we head out to meet Jen at Crandon Park Beach on Key Biscayne. With one set of diapers for land, another for sea, wipes, a lunch box, my new pee pee–proof beach blanket, sunscreen, sippy cup, and bottle, I even feel prepared.

"Look girls, isn't the water beautiful?" I ask as we drive over the causeway leading to the key.

"Wee!" shouts Isabelle.

"Gurgle, gurgle," babbles Jessica.

"Shit," I swear under my breath. From the bottom of the causeway, bumper-to-bumper traffic stretches as far as the eye can see.

"Mommy, why are there so many cars? Will we be at the beach soon? I want to see Zoe!!" says Isabelle, referring to Jen's older child.

BRRRRINNNGGGG! The cell phone rings. Jen, who is farther ahead, confirms my fear. We have driven straight into traffic for the famed Lipton Tennis Tournament.

"Mommy, is that Zoe? I want to talk to Zoe!" cries Isabelle.

"*Whaaaaa!*" screams Jessica.

Calls, back and forth, with Jen. To push on or bag it? We've made big mommy promises. We will persevere. Prayers: Please don't let Isabelle ask for a bathroom. Strategizing: Should I let her drink water? Can I slip a diaper under her from the front seat? After all, we're not moving.

BRRRRINNNGGGG! "Crandon is being used for tournament parking. Let's meet at that beach farther down instead. If you can't find me just call," says Jen, an ace under fire. I'm beginning to feel like a mom on a military campaign.

"But I want to go to the carousel at Crandon!" cries Isabelle. The carousel? Did I really mention it? Yes, days ago. Only a fool tells small kids the plans in advance.

We inch along. Jessica wants out of her car seat. Isabelle has five thousand questions. Who are all these people in shorts walking in front of our car? Why aren't we going to the carousel? Can we still go to the beach? If not, can we play tennis instead? Why not? What is tennis? A racket? Really? How big is the ball? Why are we going to the beach when everybody else is going to play tennis? Where *is* the beach?!

I talk for thirty minutes nonstop. Anything to keep my toddler's mind off the potty, or asking for water. Working in my office all week, I've been looking forward to our beach outing. Now, all I want is to get to the bathroom at the end of the key. When we finally do, without an accident, I'm so relieved that I could call it a day.

But the beach. Oh yes, the beach. Carrying Jessica and holding Isabelle's hand, I leave the restroom and walk from one end of the parking lot to the other. No sign of Jen. Yet cell phones have made modern moms near invincible. Calm and confident, I call my friend.

BEEP. BEEP. BEEP. BEEP. BEEP. Out at the end of the key, I've lost reception. The call won't go through. Yet the phone does manage to beep, indicating I have five messages. I was hoping to reconnect with my friend from Isabelle's baby group, whom I've barely seen since having a second. Now I've invited her on the playdate from hell and am not even answering her calls. Great.

"Where is Zoe!?" screams my three year old, who, having been promised the carousel, waited for the bathroom, and missed out on tennis, is heading for a breakdown.

"I don't know," I answer. And I no longer care. For back at the car, I've got a bigger problem. How do I get to the beach? I can manage all our stuff on pavement. But I forgot about the sand. Damn thing about a beach. With the baby on my hip, the lunch box and diaper bag over my shoulder, purse and beach blanket in the stroller, and toddler's hand firmly in mine, I cross the parking lot. Then I begin to drag the stroller across the sand, inch by hot inch.

Then I spy him—a big, muscle-bound fellow standing empty-handed in a bathing suit. Between the toddler, baby, and nursing dress over the tank suit, I'm not the babe he had in mind. But when I ask him to drag the stroller to a spot near the water, he doesn't dare say no.

The beach! Ah, sweet relief! I place Jessica on the sand, spread out the pee pee-proof blanket, open the lunch box, and pass Isabelle a sandwich. Finally settled, I gaze at the shimmering, aquamarine water. Maybe it was worth it after all. Then I look up to see Jen.

My friend mentions tennis, pee problems, cell-phone reception, and unanswered messages, then points to a spot down the beach. "Can you come over there? I've got someone with me. Zoe really wants to see Isabelle."

I bet.

I repack the lunch box and diaper bag, shake out and fold up the blanket, reload the stroller, put the baby back on my hip. Macho man having fled, Jen and I drag the stroller to her spot on the sand, where I unpack all over again.

We have arrived at the beach.

During the next hour, I have several piecemeal conversations with Jen—all interrupted by sunscreen applications and lifeguard duty. I change a poopy, sandy diaper. Jessica eats two mouthfuls of sand and tries to eat more. Isabelle splashes happily in the water with Zoe.

We don't stay long. We can't. It's taken all morning to get here and is almost naptime. And so, after an hour, I pack it all up again—blanket, lunch box, diapers, purse, baby, and toddler—all now covered with sand.

I'm dragging the stroller to the car when I hear a mom comment to a friend, "I'm going to the beach a lot this summer. It's so great with kids."

Yeah, maybe in five years.

Another Saturday. Bill sizes up the disheveled, frazzled woman before him, confused. "It's like the novel *A Passage to India*. The woman goes into the cave. She isn't the same when she comes out. But no one knows what happened there," says my husband. "I know you went to the park. I know there's sand at the park. I know there was sun, but I still don't get it."

How can he? Every time he takes the kids out on Sunday, he returns smiling. Every time I take them out, I come home a wreck. This morning, all started well. The very sight of the two of them strapped into our spanking new double stroller warmed my heart. Mobility! Two at a time! Strapped in, captured, all mine! Ah, the joy of the double stroller after that mile-long walk through the mall, baby on my arm, Isabelle having regressed to take Jessica's place in the old stroller. For weeks, I'd waited for the arrival of the new stroller, my Christmas present from Bill's mother. ("Don't you want something for yourself?" she'd asked. "This *is* for me," I'd responded.) We go to the park a lot during the week. But with the double stroller I figured it would be a good Saturday adventure. Bill even photographed us as we set off.

The kids enjoyed the ride over. Once there, though, Jessica quickly melted down. Some days are just no-wins. My little one didn't want to swing. She didn't want to slide. She only wanted me to stoop over, hold her two hands, and walk her around, or sit and play with her in the sand. So I've spent two hours bent over walking Jessica and another hour sitting in hot sand. I've got sand in places I didn't even know I had, baby food all over my dress. Throughout I've also been dealing with Isabelle, hoisting her up to the monkey bars, watching her go down the slide, and taking her to the bathroom. No wonder studies show that mothers hit a low point when the second child reaches eight months and becomes mobile. Dealing with a little rug rat while an older child demands attention is draining.

Making matters worse, the stroller proved a one-way thrill. Heading home, Jessica refused to sit in it, leaving me pushing Isabelle in the heat while carrying a squalling one year old—a position eerily reminiscent of the one I'd gotten the damn thing to remedy. Yet this time, it's more difficult than at the mall, because the double stroller is harder to get around corners than the single one. The double stroller might be a necessity, but I'm not going to be setting any speed records with it.

So Bill is right: a lot has happened. Yet it isn't really the sand, or even the double stroller. What's upsetting is the accumulating evidence. This Saturday finally confirms it: I'm an incredibly incompetent mother of two beyond the bounds of my own home.

I hadn't expected this. Everyone says the second child is easier, and caring for my younger daughter alone is almost pure pleasure. I feel much more confident with Jessica than I did with Isabelle and manage both pretty well at home. Fearful, I didn't bathe Isabelle for a month. Jessica was squeaky clean within days, and I dealt with the "helpful" efforts of big sister to boot. I can nurse, tell an amazing toddler tale, and pump breast milk simultaneously. I can get my big girl in her pajamas while changing the little one's diaper. In the house, I'm a paragon of productivity, and can usually even keep the trains running on time.

Leaving home with them, however, is another matter. One small child is easy to get into the car and can go almost anywhere. Two children require kid-friendly environments, and the last-minute protests to change clothes and bring toys make it almost impossible to leave the house. (Three little ones, I've heard, effectively grounds you.) With our new addition, life is all about logistics. I'm as organized as a battalion commander, but I'm clearly losing the war.

I haven't felt so hamstrung since I reported in Nicaragua and the Sandinistas, mad at losing the elections, closed the country's borders and turned off the phones and lights.

Yet Churchill's famous words, "Never give in," echo, as does his admonition, "We shall fight on the beaches. We shall fight on the landing grounds. We shall fight in the fields. . . . Never surrender!" Our two-minute conversation at the park was fairly disjointed, but seeing my friend Leslie juggle her new baby and chase her toddler made me like her more than ever. The next Saturday morning, I take the battle to my own turf and invite them over.

They arrive all smiles. It's hot. So the kids play in the house. And how they play. I never realized how much destruction two toddlers can wreak while their mothers are tending their siblings. Within a few hours, every block and building device we own is strewn on the floor. The Play-Doh is out. Stuffed animals cover three rooms. Yet in the bedroom, our toddlers end up fighting over one blue block.

It's not Leslie's fault. She's carrying a baby, and her older child is hungry and tired. We've reached that point in the tiny-tot playdate where it's all about to unravel, and once you've got momentum to leave a place with small kids, you've got to keep going. Knowing what will happen if they stay, I urge them to go. When they leave, though, the house looks like a tornado hit it.

My kids have cabin fever, having been home all day. I have an hour of cleaning up to do. And what kind of arrangement is this, anyway? You trash my house one weekend; I'll trash yours the next? I like Leslie a lot. However, the interrupted adult conversation wasn't worth the toddler clashes and mess. And the call that precedes many of these toddler playdates is irksome too. "Well, Joey has a runny nose and was up till three A.M. the other night vomiting, but I don't think he's contagious anymore. We'd be happy to come over—just wanted you to know." Usually by the second child, and certainly by the third, parents don't cancel playdates for illness, having realized how few days in life are germfree. Yet they feel compelled to make a full disclosure.

And so, what to do? Humbled by my Saturday defeats, I approach the man who returns home serene with the children each Sunday afternoon.

"What exactly are you doing on Sundays?" I ask.

"I take them to Quaker meeting and then to Spec's Music store," Bill answers.

"What else do you do?"

"I don't do anything else."

"Don't you get bored doing the same thing every week?"

"Sometimes. But it works. The Quakers are great with the kids, and Jessica and Isabelle like the music store. They often have parties there."

I have a romantic image for weekend outings with the kids. My husband has something better: a routine.

It's a week later. I no longer care about creating memories. All my charmed childhood recollections, I now realize, are from age seven and older. I don't care if we see friends. I don't care if we have fun. I just want to get them out and back without feeling like I've climbed Mount Everest. After talking to Bill, I've lowered my sights. This Saturday, all I want is a bathroom, air conditioning, and a sand-free children's area.

So imagine my delight when, at the local Borders, we find a bathroom with a changing table and a jovial man dressed up as a grasshopper reading to the kids. Grasshopper Green! Entertainment that is not me! We listen, we use the potty, and I read stories after Green finishes his routine. When I look at my watch, hours have passed. Can this be?

The following week we hit Barnes and Noble. Glory hallelujah—someone is reading again. Story time—two little words to soothe the mommy soul. It isn't long. There aren't any adult chairs. But it's an event, a destination, somebody talking besides me, and it's free. Others moms are there, and sometimes, since it's Saturday, I even compare parenting notes with a dad or two.

Borders. Barnes and Noble. Soon we're on a roll. Looking for a triple-header, we spend the next Saturday morning at our local independent store, Books and Books.

Books and Books doesn't have a changing table, but the bathroom is off the kids' section, reason enough for a visit. After a few weeks of alternating bookstores, we settle on Books and Books—not because of any highfalutin ideas about bookstore politics, but because of logistics. Story time starts earlier at Books and Books. There's a café to get an adult sandwich and bagels and juice for the kids. It's a small place where you see familiar faces from the park and can ask another parent to watch the kids while you fill the meter. It's also close to two other sources of entertainment on hot days: the car wash and the youth center, where I eventually enroll Isabelle in a Saturday morning tumbling class.

With the class, I finally get my Saturday routine down. Books and Books is at ten. Jessica and I watch Isabelle tumble at eleven. Afterwards we play at the youth center or go to the car wash, eating out of the lunch box. Then home, and Daddy's on for baths and naps.

And we do that, invariably, every Saturday, week after week, month after month. I don't see Jen. I don't see Leslie.

But I get to know the Cuban grandma at tumbling class well and become so friendly with the woman reading at Books and Books that we go to dinner together. Best of all, when I hand the kids over to Bill, exercised, fed, and entertained, I feel, finally, like the competent mother of two.

You can have the double stroller. Take the Baby Bjorn too. But don't mess with my routine.

By the time Jessica is eighteen months old, the transformation is complete. The adventuress has become a creature of habit.

In the chaos of a growing family, you're often only as good as your best routine. Discovering a workable Saturday plan made me a functional mother of two. When I found a weekday work schedule that allowed me to spend time with the kids for several hours midday, I felt like I'd won the lottery. Before having children, I'd scoffed at the routinized life. Even with one child, I'd ignored the experts' advice to follow schedules. With two, however, my little routines became sacrosanct. Once you discover the keys to the parenting kingdom, there's no turning back.

Busy mothers need a lot of no-brainers. Routines eliminate the need for planning and make it easier to manage kids, reducing negotiating time. Why can't we watch a video? Because movie night is Thursday night and it's Tuesday. Why are we going to Books and Books? Because it's Saturday. End of conversation, out the door—habit hitting its stride.

As life has gotten busier, routines have helped me as well. The fights I have with my kids are nothing compared to the debate I'd have with myself about going to the gym if it weren't automatic. I can't even imagine negotiating childcare arrangements anew with Bill and Nancy every day.

Sometimes, after going through a frustrating stretch with the kids, I'll dream of making radical life changes. Usually, though, I just need to change the routine. Soon after the girls turned two and four, bedtime became incredibly tedious. The fantasies started: an escape to a hotel, a secret haven by the beach, running away to a writer's colony. Then I cut the number of bedtime books from four to two, and life changed. As the kids had grown, their books had gotten longer, leaving Mom tired and tongue-tied by the time we got to brushing teeth.

There are downsides to all this, of course. Many friends have fallen off my radar screen, my social life consisting largely of chance encounters. Some activities don't get done at all because there's no slot for them: going to movies, shopping, and gardening, to name a few.

And, of course, I make exceptions. But with my kids still so small, I always seem to pay for these special outings with fatigue, stress, and feeling off kilter. So many things that sound like fun prove a major exercise in logistics with children under five. And once you make an exception, they think it's the rule.

Anyway, for now, boring isn't so bad. In fact, though the adventuress is loath to admit it, I like the regular days with my kids the best.

Until one day, I wake up and don't.

It's confusing at first. Jessica and Isabelle are thriving. The weather is good. Work is even going well.

Yet making the lunch box is more tedious than usual. Brushing teeth seems to take forever. Even reading the sweet stories with Jessica before Nancy comes feels monotonous. Later, at the computer, yesterday's interesting words suddenly lack meaning.

"But I love my routine," I protest to my brother, Jon, during a call.

"Routines are great, but you need to break out of them," advises Jon, my parenting consultant since he has older children.

I've had it in mind for some time. It's a beautiful day. If I leave at four, I can finish researching the magazine article before I go and beat the traffic. If my husband takes Jessica from Nancy at five-thirty, I can skip rush hour and come home at seven.

My big girl is so excited when I break the news that she can barely contain herself. "We're going to the beach?! Really? Just you and me?!"

It seems unbelievable to me too, memories of sand up my fanny having kept me from Florida's beaches for months. Going with one small child is so different than schlepping two, though.

At the beach, Isabelle chases seagulls and we laugh as one old bird pecks at the remains of a red balloon. Later we eat pasta at a big-girl restaurant all by ourselves.

It's hard to see how far you've traveled without leaving your life once in a while. Taking in the big, open horizon with my firstborn, I feel so far from home and my day-to-day life and identity.

For a few hours, at the beach, I'm that light, carefree woman of my distorted memory: the mother of one.

It's an incredibly refreshing change for a mother of two.

Double Up

Now before you dash off to story time with the little ones, let me don my advice-giver hat and provide some practical information that can make such outings work marvels for your marriage.

A little time in the trenches makes it clear that there are two main strategies for dealing with the kids during those hours when both parents are available: double up and divide and conquer. In double up, one parent takes the children, leaving the other free. In the divide-and-conquer scenario, the kids are split between the parents. What works best depends on lots of factors, including the children's ages, the activities, the time of day, and whether you're married to Cro-Magnon man or an enlightened being. My husband being the latter, we use both strategies. Yet the one that keeps us sane is double up.

The reason? Two simple words that resonate like never before: free time. With one child, free time comes automatically. There's always that nap, and when one parent steps in, the other is off duty. However, it's nearly impossible to get two or more to nap together. If one kid wants to wash the car with Daddy on Saturday, the other one will have cook-with-Mommy plans. With Isabelle, Bill and I got so used to alternating that at times I took my breaks for granted. When he departed that first Sunday with toddler and baby, however, the house felt like a temple. Redemption. Resurrection. Renewal. I got it all, and he was the one who went to church.

Not that doubling up is easy. As my Saturday strikeouts show, for wimpy moms, like me, or dads who won't flex their muscles outside the gym, it can be difficult to take the kids out alone at the beginning. Doubling up also reduces family time. Parents who work outside the home and don't see their families much during the week may be loath to part company on weekends. It's also hard to do ambitious outings with two small children without another adult, often impossible with three.

But from what I've seen, the more typical weekend scenario—alternating doing divide and conquer with time together—means that by Sunday night, neither parent has had a break. Family time often isn't as idyllic as it appears, toddler tantrums sabotaging the most promising outings. Small kids also often gravitate to Mom, despite Dad's best intentions, leaving Dad feeling left out and Mom exhausted. No wonder many working mothers' silent refrain is "Thank God it's Monday!" and stay-at-home moms count the hours until preschool like rosary beads.

All couples have to figure out what works for them, but I have yet to meet a mother beyond one who couldn't use more free time. So for those interested in doubling up, at least occasionally, here are some tips Bill and I hashed out on a date night. May they spare you the expensive arguments, so you can savor dinner instead.

Formalize It. When you leave with the kids, say when you'll be back. This we learned after a massive case of project interuptus with our first, when Bill returned earlier than expected with Isabelle. I'd just gotten out the potting soil. Our toddler quickly spread the dirt all over the patio, and two or more makes for a real mudfest. Specifying a return time allows your spouse to plan. Nothing is more ridiculous than getting angry at your husband, who took the kids out, for coming back too soon. Believe me, I know.

Scheduling also helps. If Saturday afternoon is Daddy's time, it's easier to plan ahead. It's disconcerting and frustrating to suddenly have an hour—a whole hour!—free and fritter part of it away figuring out which pressing task to do. Planning allows parents to think ahead about free time and outings. For couples like us, with only one car, it's essential.

We've also found it useful to tell the kids who is going to be "in charge." When Daddy covers Saturday afternoon while I work in my office upstairs, he's in charge. When I cover and he does yoga in the bedroom on Sunday afternoon, I am. This lets the kids know who to ply with requests to decorate the house with paper napkins and toilet paper. Better yet, it establishes who cleans up afterward.

Because of such projects, we've found it best to have one parent take the kids out for at least part of each day. They get exercise and stimulation. Our house stays clean, and the person at home is left in peace. When Jessica and Isabelle are home, they're usually involved in a creative endeavor, such as getting out all the kitchenware for an imaginary party or dressing up in Mommy's nightgowns. While cute, these projects require massive cleanup.

For some parents, doubling up is part of a broader effort to equally divide duties. If so, be concrete. As *Halving It All* notes, fifty-fifty is in some ways the easiest parental arrangement because it's so clear-cut. To make it work, though, we've learned that you need to be specific. With our first, Bill and I agreed to do the same amount of childcare and even tracked hours. I also put all those invisible details—from planning birthday parties and buying kids' clothes to researching schools and scheduling doctors' appointments—on a list, and we divided them up. Doing this with the first made our transition to the second much easier than it would have been otherwise. Things are far looser now, but only because we've agreed on the rules of the game.

If this sounds anal, consider: Is there any parent who isn't keeping track of their spouse's free time anyway? Golfers' wives know exactly how long that game takes. Better negotiation than resentment. Men are good at dealing with specifics. Vague requests for "more help" are hard to satisfy. Passive aggression, I've found, is even less effective.

Treat Yourself. By Jessica's birth, I realized that the real challenge isn't negotiating free time with my spouse, who's a generous and enlightened man. The real challenge is negotiating with myself over how to use the hours he gives me.

After a few bad episodes, when Bill returned expecting gratitude and instead encountered resentment because I'd used my "free" time to clean and pay bills, I made a personal deal: one or two chores first, then self-indulgence. Simple is best. Painting my toenails to Beethoven when I had two toddlers made me feel like a diva. Potting a plant without a little helper is divine. The surest way to marital hell is to spend your free time cleaning his side of the closet because you found your shoes under his jeans.

Some people assume that stay-at-home moms have free time during the week and therefore don't need it on the weekend—after all, it's the husband who "works," and if you haven't been there much, the park sounds like a jaunt. Actually, these moms (and in some cases dads) often need a break even more than their mates. As anyone who spends time alone with two little ones quickly realizes, staying at home with small kids is a full-time job, rewarding and important, yet harder than most. Women who do it are more depressed than women who work outside of the home (with the exception of full-time working moms who get little help from their spouses, whom one study found to be more depressed). Trading the kids back and forth on weekends recognizes that both partners work during the week. If he can't take the children out, then leave yourself. There's no mom—or wife—as good as a rejuvenated one.

Don't Ask, Don't Tell. Refrain from criticizing Dad upon his return. What you don't know can't hurt you. What you don't like, you can't change. Bubble gum in a child's hair can be hard to take, I know. But it's a small price for freedom. Let him do things his way. My husband, for one, has made it clear that he's a lot happier to take the kids when he doesn't have to return to face the Grand Inquisitor.

This, of course, is easier said than done. Oh, how, on occasion, I've wanted to take over! When Jessica was a year old, Bill and I started alternating putting the kids to bed. His first night on, I thought my little one would never stop wailing. Our experience with Isabelle, however, kept me from intervening: I've never seen my husband madder than when I've interfered when he's supposed to be in charge. So I gritted my teeth through Jessica's crying phase. It passed quickly, though, and the break from the night shift was worth it. Today Bill routinely puts them to bed with only two time-outs each. (I like the white foam earplugs with the twenty-nine-decibels noise-reduction rating.)

Express Gratitude. Finally, don't forget to thank your mate for taking the kids out. Dig out that old lacy black thing. Make him lunch. Compliment his bulging biceps—whatever it takes. Reinforcement is critical. The popular wisdom is that dads who spend time with their kids get lots of strokes. In fact, while the women at the park may admire your husband, they probably won't talk to him. Fathers who do a lot of childcare often feel alienated and isolated. In addition to being the odd man on the mommy circuit, they often have to listen to men who've put their careers well ahead of their kids brag about their promotions and get kudos just for attending the ballet recital. And employers are often even less supportive of men's domestic contributions than they are of women's.

Okay, I need to practice what I preach. I don't even own a lacy black thing.

But it's good advice, isn't it?

The Amazing Toddler Diet

The best thing about little kids is that they never finish their food—so you get to eat it!

—MY MOTHER, who, unlike her daughter, never let this little fact affect her figure

October. Jessica is five months old. The gym scale says I weigh 216 pounds.

Now it's one thing to be heavy. I've always been at least a little overweight. A big-boned, five-foot-eight mother, I can get away with carrying more weight than many women. Even before kids, I hit a high of 180, liberated from dieting by marrying a man who accepted me, Häagen-Dazs and all.

But 216 pounds is different. How did this happen? I started my second pregnancy with some padding from the first, and with my eye on the toddler instead of the mirror, I ate less carefully. Once again, nursing has put weight on rather than sucked it off. Five months after Jessica's birth, I've lost only 12 of my 42 pregnancy pounds. But 216 pounds?

It's a frightening moment on the scale, but not because I look like a Teletubby. Appearance, after years with spit-up on my blouse and jelly stains on my shoes, is not the issue. The problem is that walking has become painful. Some two-hundred-plus pounds, one large baby or squirming toddler, diaper bag, purse, and lunch box stresses even size-nine feet. Recently I've developed a painful heel condition. Soaking my feet every night, I worry: how am I going to chase after my kids, much less carry them?

The jig is up. I need to lose at least fifty pounds.

But the diets in *Glamour* and *Self* no longer fit my life. I've now got four birthday party invitations on the bulletin board, whole milk in the fridge, and cookies to bring to the preschool party. At story time that little fellow with the rumbly in his tumbly beckons: "Just a little smackeral?"

Motherhood is fattening, and more so with each child. You can take one kid to adult restaurants. Two puts you at the pizza parlor. Then there are the birthday parties, holiday treats, and preschool party trays—doubled. Now that we're a bigger clan and less mobile, family comes to visit us for the holidays. After my second, I realized: Christmas is just *four* weeks after Thanksgiving. And this time the leftovers are in my fridge. No wonder a recent study found that a woman's risk of obesity increases by 7 percent for each child she has and that a man's goes up 4 percent.

I didn't eat much kiddie food with my first or change many of my eating habits. However, a growing family makes for bigger culinary ambitions. Waffles and french toast drenched in syrup are now regular breakfast items, stuff I haven't eaten since my mother made them for me. Running a finger through the syrup has also passed from mother to daughter, along with its dictum: if you lick it off your finger, the calories don't count. Add to that family-size peanut butter—I don't know why, Jessica's not even old enough to eat it—and the stress of getting two little ones to bed. By nine P.M., they are calling me: crackers smothered with cream cheese and jelly.

Still, if motherhood is fattening, it's also motivating—more than any man, any magazine, or even my own mother has ever been. Obese people have shorter, less healthy lives. I have two small but very compelling reasons to be fit. And what better way to teach my kids healthy eating habits than by modeling them?

Yet to lose weight with children, you have to use motherhood to your advantage. So as the months go by, I perfect it: the Amazing Toddler Diet. Here then, for the first time, is the only weight-loss plan that recognizes that the biggest challenge for a dieting mom is not the little ones but the toddler within, helping you take her on with the skills you've acquired as a parent.

Get a program and make it a routine. Like all toddlers, the muncher within needs structure. Soon after hitting 216, I went on the Weight Watchers program. Weight Watchers is great because it's positive. There are no "bad" foods—you eat what you want, and there is no way I'm going to drink dinner out of a can while dishing out dollops of love to others. For if the psychologists assert that food is not love, we mommies know better. Food, absolutely, is love. How else to explain all of that baking?

With Weight Watchers you count food points. My limit when I start is 29 points, which, early on, are used up by afternoon. Counting points after years on the mommy track is a revelation: I'm amazed to discover how high calorie my diet has become. Pregnant, I gave up nonfat yogurt to avoid artificial sweeteners, switching to the sugar-sweetened, low-fat variety. Isabelle prefers whole milk to 2 percent. Now I do too. Forced to write down everything I put in my mouth, I also realize how much is unconsciously going in: sandwich crusts, half-eaten birthday cake, barely nibbled buns. By changing to low-fat cereals and nonfat yogurts, and refraining from cleaning the toddler plate, I lose two pounds in the first two weeks alone.

It's best to attend Weight Watchers meetings. After going to a few, though, I stop, unable to fit them in my schedule. Yet the early ones provide a foundation, and I continue the program on my own. After counting points for a few weeks, I change my eating habits and don't need to count them every day, my new food choices having become as routinized as bedtime is for my kids.

Manage your inner toddler like you do your little ones, setting rules and sticking to them. "Maybe" is music to the ears of my inner toddler. Like my kids, she's an expert negotiator, arguing that licking the peanut butter off the knife saves money. So no is no. I seal my lips before birthday parties. It's difficult to eat at these affairs anyway, with sticky fingers in your food and your firstborn pulling on your dress to complain that the hostess won't share her dolls.

Avoiding confrontation works with the inner toddler as well. I do not put candy in front of Isabelle and Jessica. And I no longer bring home desserts for skinny Bill, who forgets to eat them anyway—mine is the willpower of a two year old. My memory may be faulty, but it's photographic concerning the refrigerator's contents.

Distraction also works well. Focusing on the conversation rather than the food at social events, for instance, can help. The mother with the frosting on her finger at the birthday party isn't really listening, but she's there, she's amiable, and talking to her—even about schools—is better than doing what she's doing. Silently playing "I spy" at these events is also beneficial. I spy an overweight mommy finishing her son's hot dog. I spy a skinny one who hasn't noticed the cake. I spy four Weight Watchers points on the fork of the twins' mother.

And call it an incentive program if you don't like the word "bribe." Isabelle gets a sticker if she's ready for school on time. Mommy's reward for losing fifty pounds is a bracelet—one of the few things that will still fit if I lose more, as I hope to.

Preen and play. Still, every mom knows the best toddler management tool is fun. Making dieting at least amusing can coax the inner toddler along and keep her active too. To that end:

- *Buy toys*. The kids have a plastic slide and wagons. What about Mom? For many women it's impossible to get to the gym after the birth of another child. Exercise must be convenient. A double jogger changed my editor's life. Another mom friend has her own exercise machine. The parenting magazines show new moms hoisting babies in various exercise positions, but free weights squirm less and don't drool.

- *Play dress up*. My toddlers have Cinderella and Ariel outfits. I play dress up in my own closet, dreaming of wearing outfits from previous lives. They may be my former "fat jeans," but they're fantasy clothes now.

■ *Make it interesting*. The experts claim otherwise, but the chubby inner toddler knows that food is fun. And if being fat isn't great, getting fat is divine. Chips, seconds on desserts, crackers drenched in dip . . . what a ride!

Losing weight is never going to be as fun as gaining it. However, as with kids' chores, adding novelty can make it tolerable. After I fell off the wagon, Weight Watchers' online program made counting points interesting enough for me to purge the peanut butter again. Like Isabelle with her projects, I also often throw out a half-filled notebook and start counting points anew with one that is bright purple, pink, or green. The thrill lasts five minutes, but it gets me started.

And when all else fails, I throw Isabelle on the bed. Chasing Jessica in a good game of "I'm going to get you" helps too. No wonder it's taken all these years to lose weight. Few things are as fun as food. Luckily, playing with children is one of them.

Fool the picky eater. Mothers often use little tricks to get small children to eat right: witness the ketchup on the eggs, peanut butter on the banana. The munchy inner toddler can be tricked too. Fiber, for instance, is the great freebie of dieting. The body has to work harder to digest high-fiber wheat bread than it does a baguette, for instance, making the former a better choice than the later for losing weight. Wasa crackers, with two grams of fiber apiece, are great, whole-wheat pasta a good choice too. The baguette bought to occupy the toddler in the shopping cart has to go, but she never ate as much of it as I did anyway.

Other great tricks: a mister for olive oil on salads, and chocolate biscotti for Mommy-needs-a-treat nights, the latter only three Weight Watcher points compared to five for the brownie from school. Another favorite: I Can't Believe It's Not Butter! spray, which has no points and is divine on vegetables and air-popped popcorn. Sometimes with a bigger family, you need not just to buy, but also to eat, in bulk. When the biscotti is too small after a tiny-tot bedtime siege, a huge bowl of popcorn soothes the mommy soul. My kids like the popcorn and spray too.

Treat all the toddlers the same. Dieting is supposed to be a way of life, not a crash, six-week affair. For a mom, this means finding foods and strategies that work for the whole family—in other words, getting not just a diet but a life. This sounds contradictory at first. Aren't the kids the problem? In fact, what's good for the adults also benefits children, helping them establish healthy habits. It's also easier if everyone is on the same program. Who has time to prepare special diet food? To this end:

■ *Turn off the TV*. On this issue, parenting and diet experts agree: Television makes all of us, young and old, fat. The American Academy of Pediatrics discourages television viewing for children under two years. The phrase "couch potato" says it all for adults.

■ *Eat before you go*. If possible, feed everybody before the birthday party. By eating with my girls before one kiddie bash, I was able to pass up the following: make-your-own pizza with three kinds of cheese, salad drenched in oil, cake, ice cream, and chips. My kids also got something in their stomachs besides sugar and fat for the afternoon.

■ *Skip the juice*. Big business has convinced mothers that children cannot survive without juice. The dentists and nutritionists, however, say juice just gives kids cavities and makes them fat. I have to drink a third of the juice box before handing it to the toddler to keep it from splattering out of the straw. Whole fruit is healthier and more filling.

Soon after I started my diet, I stopped buying juice boxes. After a few complaints from my kids, I never heard much more about them. When we go out to dinner, we all drink "sparkly water," as my girls call Perrier. When I do have juice, I cut the calories by mixing it with club soda and feel as bubbly as my toddler in her bath.

■ *Use big-girl manners*. How I expected Jessica to learn to eat with a fork when I was using my fingers, I'm not sure. Manners are clearly good for adults too. If you don't put it in a bowl, at least put it on a plate. No smackerals—unless you want to look like Winnie-the-Pooh.

Learn from your kids. If toddlers pose a challenge to dieting, some of their behavior is also actually useful to model, including:

■ *Eat five or six small meals a day*. Notice the day-care schedule: snack at eleven, lunch at twelve-thirty, and another snack at three. The experts say we should eat many small meals during the day—just like little kids do. Using the children's bowl also makes portions look bigger.

■ *Take toddler-size steps*. When Jessica was learning to walk, no one suggested that she jog around the block. Returning to the gym after having my second child, out of shape and busier than ever, I developed the shortest exercise routine of any regular: thirty minutes six days a week for the bike and stretching, and a little extra for weights when I've got time. Okay, sometimes it's twenty minutes, even fifteen. Yet half of life is showing up, and there's a huge difference between something and nothing—twenty minutes for the inner toddler is long! The trainers say you won't accomplish anything with such a pathetic routine, but this isn't true and just puts off a lot of busy parents. If my mom friends realized how short my exercise routine is they'd be a lot more likely to work out themselves. Weight training, especially, can produce big results in little time.

Weight Watchers' exercise goals are modest and can be achieved by doing activities like gardening and housework. Wednesdays, for me, is the "Winn-Dixie" workout at our local supermarket.

■ *Get back up after you fall down*. Toddlers fall, get back up, and carry on. The first holiday season on the Amazing Toddler Diet, I had momentum. By the second, I'd been eating Wasa crackers and air-blown popcorn for more than a year. And our holiday season is long—Thanksgiving is followed by Nancy's birthday in early December, Christmas, New Year's, and, finally, Isabelle's birthday in January.

I don't know how it happened. We only had twelve people to Isabelle's fourth birthday party. When they left, though, I was sitting with the remains of a princess cake for thirty. After stuffing the piñata, filling the goody bags, and buying the presents, I deserved it. . . .

Wipeout.

It took me five pounds and lots of foot soaking to start counting points again. But I did, motivated by the same thing that initially got me started: two wiggle worms who want to roughhouse and have no tolerance for a slow-footed mom.

Find support. Finally, who can imagine a toddler taking her first steps without applause? Support is critical to the inner tot as well.

Showing up at 216 in nursing tops and maternity pants made an impression. I can't attend the Weight Watchers meetings, but I develop a fan club at the gym. As my weight slowly drops, people I've never noticed pull me aside for kudos. The older Cuban men are so complimentary that at 190, I start to feel chic.

Then there's Jerry, a nice-looking fellow, who calls me "skinny" when I'm still anything but. One day, discouraged after the princess-cake binge, I'm pumping iron as he runs past. "Hey," he shouts, "you're really looking buff!"

Buff? After two pregnancies, years of breast-feeding, and double duty on the peanut butter–and-jelly shift? I can do another weight machine, buy more high-fiber crackers, and eat before the birthday party.

It takes a long time for vanity to kick in again. Bill has shot me in the butt with fertility drugs, seen my ovaries in surgery, and stuck with me through my worst mommy moods. His love is unconditional. I can't do it for him.

However, my muscular fans at the gym finally have me examining my tush in the mirror one night, as vain as Jessica preening over her Belle costume.

Initially, I wanted to lose weight to keep up with my kids. Now, spotting my hipbones, I want to be a princess too.

Two years on the Amazing Toddler Diet. Two years of eating carrots and high-fiber crackers. Six months of those two years on a plateau.

"Lost a lot of weight chasing the girls around?" a neighbor asks one day.

Please!

October. Jessica is two and a half. The medical scale at the gym reads 166 pounds.

Motherhood is such a mushy occupation, all those little accomplishments—finding the lost sippy cup, getting the Band-Aid on right—so infinitely immeasurable at the end of the day.

But fifty pounds is big, solid, quantifiable—the weight of two toddlers combined.

I step on the scale. I step off.

No problem.

I can write a book.

Bring in the Bears

Outnumbered.

Single parents with more than one child face this dilemma all the time, couples with three or more too. I feel it most when Bill is out of town. On his second night away, I'm dreading bedtime. Jessica is almost one. Isabelle is three. Last night's toddler tears and time-outs left me exhausted before I'd even started kitchen and garbage duty. Are the childcare manuals only for parents of singletons? Suddenly discipline techniques that worked perfectly well before my second's birth are failing. With Jessica on my hip, Isabelle's time-out was harder on me than it was on big sister last night.

Yet tonight I'm determined to take control. Bracing myself, I approach Isabelle at eight P.M. in the living room. "Time to put on your pajamas," I say, Jessica on my shoulder.

Isabelle runs to her room and throws on her tutu. Then she begins prancing through the house.

Realizing that I'm going to need both hands, I carry Jessica to the kitchen, prepare a bottle, and then leave my baby on the floor of Isabelle's room with it. My firstborn is now in our bedroom. "Isabelle, bedtime!" I shout, heading there. Big sister refuses to remove the tutu.

After checking on Jessica, I return to our bedroom, where Isabelle is now doing toddler cartwheels. My older child is a natural gymnast. She didn't get it from me, though. Chasing her, I hear God laughing.

"Okay, I'm going to start counting." One, two, three—it worked so well just a year ago.

On three my oldest whips off the tutu and begins doing arabesques. Definitely the moment for a time-out. Ah—but you can't leave a baby alone on the floor of a three year old's room! Racing to check Jessica, I find the bottle drained and my infant eating Kleenex. Bill and I disagree over whether a small child can choke on paper; I say she can. Pulling the tissue out of Jessica's mouth, I give her a toy, then run back to our bedroom and begin counting again. "One, two, three . . ." Isabelle starts jumping on our bed.

"Time-out!" I announce, running first to put Jessica in her crib, then racing back to cart Isabelle off to a living-room chair.

Isabelle usually sits in time-out, then cooperates. Not tonight. With time-out over, my firstborn leaps out of the chair and races again through the house. Meanwhile, Jessica, who I've abandoned to deal with her big sister, starts wailing in the crib. Leaving my little one sobbing to chase my big one, I definitely feel like the wrong person is being punished.

At nine P.M., neither daughter has her pajamas on, and a discipline technique perfected through an entire year of terrible twos has unraveled. I finally get them to bed by yelling at Isabelle. This works; however, it leaves me so depressed that I lick three big slabs of peanut butter off the knife after packing

Isabelle's lunch box for school. Having two children has made me a general, but I'm losing the campaign.

Yet where to get reinforcements?

Bedtime, a night later. I want a battalion. I've got a bear. Necessity *is* the mother of invention. Scrutinizing Nancy's adept handling of the girls earlier, I noticed something: she's incredibly amusing. Now, as Isabelle jumps on her tricycle instead of getting on her pajamas, I put Jessica on my hip, grab the stuffed animal, and start grunting. "Isabelle, Paddington is looking for you!" I shout, waving the bear. Excited, my first-born races after me to her room, where we find the stuffed animal daring Isabelle to put on her pajamas. Within thirty seconds my three year old is dressed for bed.

Time to brush teeth. Isabelle wants to eat Cheerios, peanut butter, and orange juice, in that order, in her pink tutu. "It might take a little while," she remarks coyly. "But it's okay."

No way. Dressed in a raincoat and boots, Paddington shrieks that it's about to storm in the house. Then, as we try to set him straight, the Barbie toothbrush calls. Isabelle races to the bathroom and brushes away. Off for a bedtime story. It's nine P.M., my mouth is tired, but Isabelle's is clean, and Jessica is so amused that when I've put her down, she hasn't even noticed the tissue on the floor. The peanut-butter-slathered knife goes straight in the sink.

With my first child, I agonized about doing things right, viewing the toddler years as an opportunity to establish my authority. Without another child to distract me, I monitored time-outs with the vigilance of a cop. But a bigger family demands new tactics. Though much of the advice in the parenting tomes no longer seems to work, one technique is clan-friendly: distraction.

I didn't fully appreciate the power of this approach with one child. However, a few nights with Paddington convinces me that silliness is now my salvation. How else to deal with such ridiculous, no-win situations than by becoming absurd yourself? At least amusing Isabelle keeps her in the same room as Jessica. Enforcing a time-out with a toddler while caring for a baby, I'm getting more exercise than I do at the gym. Tactics that worked with one, such as turning off a video, become unfair with two, punishing both sisters.

And so, over time, I become a silly mom. It doesn't look good, but that's the point: on occasion I act so ridiculous that my little ones forget their battle plans. One evening, when Isabelle refuses to read books with Bill, for instance, I say, "Okay. I'll put Daddy in the garbage can," and leave the room. Laughing, my daughter runs after her father.

There are downsides to this strategy. For one, it's easier to start some games than to finish them. In a recent effort to get the tutu off and her dress on, I started telling Isabelle what different animals eat. After discussing dogs, cats, and cows, I got stuck. What do the worms eat? Frogs? Elephants? Help! I've also learned to restrain myself around other children. Jessica and Isabelle are used to my antics, but tots with more serious moms can't tell when I'm kidding. "You have magical powers?! Really?!" exclaims one of Isabelle's friends, wide-eyed, before I set him straight.

Being amusing also gets tiring. Some nights I'm so slack-jawed after speaking for Paddington that I can barely talk to my spouse. Yet it's no more exhausting than issuing fruitless commands, or trying to clean those pearly whites when their owner won't open her mouth. On the nights when the stuffed animals fall silent, too tired for shenanigans, I often later regret my lassitude, realizing that a little absurdity early on would have made life easier.

Furthermore, it's a lot more enjoyable being a clown than a general, especially when, as the latter, you're so often on the verge of losing the war. I wanted a bigger family to have fun. If I'd wanted to give orders, I would have joined the army.

No parent should have to entertain a child all the time. I still use time-outs, usually more successfully than that weekend when my husband was away. Recently, when Paddington interrupted a particularly tearful time-out that Bill had given Isabelle, my husband protested that I'd picked the wrong moment for humor. He was right. Since then I've been careful not to let silliness interfere with discipline.

Yet as any parent beyond one knows, time-outs only further delay an already creeping family train and can be impossible to enforce with a baby onboard. And in any case, most of my battles have less to do with obedience than with conflicting agendas: mine to keep a schedule, theirs to explore the world. Why put on your pajamas when you can ride your tricycle in your tutu and it's only forty-eight o'clock?

However, when the animals start talking, bedtime looks less like an order than an invitation. And once my daughter joins my magical mystery tour, it's amazing how quickly the tricycle and tutu are forgotten.

Things look different to me as well. For one, I no longer feel so outnumbered. All those bears and Beanie Babies Grandma sent finally have a purpose, serving as valuable allies rather than clutter. Even the catalogs start to make sense. Yes, I bought the bath colors. And you will too when you hear how bath time can be transformed from a battleground to a splash of ever-changing rainbow hues. Is the water going to be green? Red? Blue? It's enough to make a three year old forget that she hates getting wet.

Some of us, of course, are more naturally ridiculous than others. My husband's attempts to make the Barbie talk amuse his wife far more than his daughters. But I like being absurd. The idea of putting the baby-sitter in a diaper makes me laugh too. And call me the sheriff who can't shoot straight, but I often have more control over my little ones when we're in cahoots than when I'm in command.

Yesterday, when Isabelle balked leaving preschool, I was about to count to three when her eyes suddenly lit up.

"I've got to go," she exclaimed, dashing past her teacher. "I've got a bear who thinks it's raining in the house!"

And, with that, we headed for home, that unpredictable place where these days, almost anything can happen anytime.

The Right Stuff

Preparing for my first child's arrival, I scrambled to buy the right baby stuff. After analyzing the difference between Pampers and Huggies, I splurged on the former. I bought mobiles in bright colors and developmentally appropriate black and white. Perusing the baby catalogs, I marked every other page. My husband and I spent an entire Saturday night setting up the baby play yard. When Isabelle actually used it, I thought the mommy tide had turned.

By the time Jessica arrived, the play yard we used for two weeks had spent two years in the garage. With a few exceptions, like the bath colors, much in the kiddie catalogs now looked comic, my quest to solve parenting's challenges with things quixotic, spendthrift, and naïve. Few of the items we'd gotten for Isabelle had had any staying power. And somehow, we'd accumulated so many—ten rubber duckies alone now inhabited our house, and none lived in the bath. This time, I needed to purge, not accumulate, kids' stuff; visit the Container Store, not Toys"R"Us.

God gave me a second girl to take advantage of the beautiful wardrobe my mother-in-law provided my first one, and as a new mom, I'd even used the spot remover to keep it sparkly.

My stuff, in contrast, was in pathetic shape. After Isabelle's explorations, batches of earrings lacked partners. Lipsticks lay decapitated. Three watches had died in the bath. The few clothes that still fit were stained with mushed banana, milk, and Play-Doh.

This time, I needed stuff not for baby, but for me. Yet no one buys a woman expecting her second a pretty nightie. (With the third, it's even worse: they just ask if you're crazy.) So during Jessica's first year, I treated myself to a few key items:

New Panties. Five months after Jessica's birth, I realized I'd been wearing maternity underwear for three years. "Wow, it goes up past your belly button," Isabelle noted in awe one morning, remarking on my panties. My bras varied so much in style and size that they looked like they belonged to Sybil of the sixteen personalities; from the contents of my underwear drawer I could have been committed. And despite the incredibly wide selection, nothing actually fit.

Shirley Jackson, who wrote books on motherhood as well as her famous short story "The Lottery," noted this phenomenon as early as 1948, and how it worsened with each child. Said Jackson, who had four: "Parents must automatically resign themselves to wearing every article of their own clothing at least two years beyond its normal life expectancy." Since then, of course, an entire revolution has passed, giving women a greater sense of entitlement. Yet the sixties feminists had it wrong: burning bras isn't the way to liberation, buying new ones is. I don't have time for a makeover. But I have a right, even an obligation to future generations, to buy new underwear.

I'd like to say I bought thongs, but that would have been like trying to squeeze an elephant into a bikini (and who wants to read about a mom beyond one who wiggles her butt right back into a thong?). Instead, most of my new panties still covered my belly button. The bras had not a shred of lace.

Yet they were clean and soft, and miraculously, they fit. It's not fun to sort through the supersizes. However, when I brought my silky loot home, I felt like a new woman.

The Coffee Thermos. Coffee is my one divine pleasure—like wine is for many of my friends, and massage is for others. I drink two cups a day and savor every sip. I can't imagine life without coffee—especially motherhood without coffee.

With Isabelle, I could maintain this obsession. It wasn't ideal, but once she sat on my hip, I could make my morning cup with one hand. During her first year, Isabelle was the perfect café buddy, napping just long enough for me to savor my brew and scan the headlines. Over time, she even developed a coteric of fans among the local baristas. On other occasions, I managed adult conversation with friends while Isabelle played with napkins. My café life hadn't been so good since I was single.

I took Jessica to a café exactly once—to meet my friend Chris and her new second baby. We had a great time and vowed we would do it again—which we never did. With Jessica it was just harder to get out. Chris and I both returned to work sooner than we had after our first births. Life also got busier—if I left the house, it was usually to do errands. A haven with one baby, the café proved an obstacle course with two toddlers. When I took the girls to Starbucks at ages three and one,

I spent most of my time wiping up spilt orange juice and saying "shhh."

Still, I could accept that my café days were over; that life now seemed incredibly decadent anyway. What bothered me, though, after Jessica arrived was that I couldn't drink a decent cup of coffee at home. With two kids, the free hand that sipped and poured was occupied. When I managed to make a cup, I was so busy bouncing up and down to find missing shoes that it went cold.

A tiny irritation, but it wore on me, especially as I warmed Jessica's milk to the perfect temperature. And I soon noticed that it bothered other mothers as well. Meeting me for a rare lunch out, a woman from India with two kids sank into her chair and stated that she'd spent her whole morning trying to drink her brew. A friend with girls older than mine arrived for story time at the local bookstore complaining that she'd heated up her morning coffee four times and had still not finished it. With two kids, I now understood the code: friend, I haven't had a moment to myself.

Now, I recognize that interruptions are part of life these days—actually, they are life. Yet, every mom needs a treat to carry her through, and my nails aren't worth a manicure.

With my thermos, I leave my coffee on the counter, give a bath, and return for a swig of self that's still steamy. Some small adult pleasure has been preserved.

I sip, therefore I am.

The Perfect Purse. For some women it's shoes, for others clothes. I begin each phase of life with a new purse. The shelf in my closet is littered with bags from former lives. There's the stylish briefcase I carried to work at *The Wall Street Journal*, about as useful in my current life as the suits that went with it. There's the leather backpack from reporting in Central America. LeSportsac with the zipper pockets marked Isabelle's entry to toddlerhood. When you've got feet problems and wear size nine wide, a purse rather than a shoe fetish is the way to go.

So, setting out to find a bag to match the demands of life with my growing family, I looked first in my closet. As with my bras, the selection was wide, yet nothing fit.

LeSportsac was too small for schlepping two kids and too squishy and therefore difficult to find things in, as I realized nearly running a red light retrieving a sippy cup. Miami is car country, so a backpack didn't make much sense. I didn't want multiple bags, slinging a diaper bag with the LeSportsac or switching from a big kiddie bag to a smaller adult one. Working at home, I have a life that's not neatly divided. In the mommy world one hour, out of it the next, I needed one bag to handle all my identities. And I didn't want to spend money on any new kiddie-type bag, keenly aware, or at least hoping, that lugging children's stuff was a phase.

The purse needed to be big and strong enough to carry diapers, sippy cups, wipes, sweaters in winter, umbrellas in summer, baby tapes for the car, and Barbie—when she refused to stay home. It needed to hold my brush, wallet, cell phone, notepad, pens, and almonds—the last being essential for passing up the more decadent treats at birthday parties. I wanted an inner divider to carry preschool art and manuscript drafts. No less than three big outer pockets for two sippy cups and my water bottle would do. Finally, I needed an inside zipper pocket for stashing tiny treasures from the park such as broken barrettes and doll arms, as well as that essential toddler tool: the sugarless bubblegum bribe.

These qualifications eliminated every purse at the local mall. Most of the bags, while perfect for one, were too small or delicate for life with two young children. Many of the bigger totes slouched so much that items placed in them disappeared completely. Most critically, almost all the purses lacked sufficient pockets. Those they did have were usually inside the bag, making them hard to find. The bags were all stylish, but this wasn't even a qualification, function having triumphed over form. If, with my first child, a purse had still been a fashion accessory, it was now more like camping gear.

The Walking Company had a perfect bag: lightweight, upright, and reasonably priced, with sufficient pockets. But the handles didn't fit over my shoulders. This seemed incredibly stupid. When it's raining and you need to carry baby and umbrella with one hand and hold the toddler's arm with the other to cross the street, all the gear has to go on the shoulder.

My quest for the perfect purse appeared hopeless until I hit the Coach store. I've never bought a designer bag before, rarely even ventured into the Coach store. Yet when I saw the black tote with the four big outer pockets, sturdy shoulder straps, and file divider proudly standing upright, it was love at first sight.

Okay, it's not really a file divider. Technically, the purse is a diaper bag: the inner divider holds a separate changing pad. With my second child I was way beyond carrying a changing pad, however, and put it aside. Without the pad, the purse quickly transformed into a serious tote, the divider holding manila files and the bag's swank black exterior making it as good for business trips as for the playground.

And when I slid the sippy cups, water, and cell phone in the outer pockets, and found Jessica's doll before the stoplight changed, I felt like a sophisticated schlepper.

(Coach no longer makes this awesome tote, but it's often on eBay, in black or khaki. May you pay less than I did or find one at Target that works just as well.)

The Palm Pilot. Packing for vacation after Jessica's birth, I realized that either the Franklin Planner or the baby was going to have to be left behind. I was sorry to abandon my paper organizer. But there was no way the bulging notebook was going to fit with all the new kiddie gear on the plane. So I bought a Palm Pilot.

I soon discovered that the Palm had other advantages besides being small. One child is a relationship. Two is a small business. The Palm is perfect for dealing with life as a mommy manager. The repeat function automatically programs in my glorious routine, from ballet lessons to pediatrician's appointments. Search locates those elusive details like the name of that other preschooler's mother when "Hello, Michelle's mom" will no longer do. With the Palm, I type in "Michelle" and, if I've entered it, her mother's name appears, giving me the feeling that she, like me, is still a separate, identifiable person.

The Palm is also a mind cleanser. Women are said to experience that exalted creative state known as "flow" less often than do men. But then, men don't sit down to work and think, *Buy size-four diapers.* The Palm's desktop program allows me to flip from my work and dump all those brain-clogging details that have doubled since Jessica's birth on its own to-do list. It's also a good place to maintain a fantasy life. "Go away for night with Bill" has been on there for several years.

During Jessica's baby phase, I got nerdy and put a flip cover with a voice recorder on my Palm. When a mom gave me the name of a divine hotel she'd spent a night at alone with her husband, I moved Jessica to my hip, pulled out the Palm, and recorded it.

The mother of three looked down at my hand, gasped, and said, "I need that!"

I thought she was admiring the bracelet I'd gotten after my first child's birth.

But she wanted the gadget I'd gotten after having my second.

A Stopwatch. Time for work was scarce with one kid. Two, however, raised the distinct possibility that the details and distractions of life would prevent me from ever writing again.

It wasn't just that I had more interruptions: I had whole new categories of them. A year before Jessica's birth, we'd bought our first house. The handyman now showed up regularly during the morning writing hours. In addition to having a new baby, there were Jessica's little friends—their moms and sitters knocking at the door and always welcome. We screen our calls. Yet now that Isabelle was in preschool, I couldn't ignore the messages. A fall off the monkey bars? Head injury? Flu? It didn't happen often—but enough to make me listen to every call. Busier himself, Bill also started working more at home, a fact that any wife can tell you is both a blessing and a curse. And though Nancy took the kids out, she also spent time with them in the house.

Virginia Woolf long ago cited the "world's notorious indifference" to the writer's work—and she didn't even have children. Noted Woolf in *A Room of One's Own*: "It does not ask people to write poems and novels and histories; it does not need them." The handyman's knock and the preschool medical forms, however, will not wait.

So after a few unsuccessful writing sessions, I turned for guidance to one of my favorite books: *A Writer's Time* by Kenneth Atchity. Soon after, I bought a new watch and started using his stopwatch method of time management.

Atchity advises using a stopwatch to "steal time" to write. His technique proved perfect for managing the multiple identities, conflicting worlds, and memory lapses of the busy parent who works at home. While my stopwatch is running, I do not send out birthday invitations. I do not pick up toys. I do not read the forwarded emails from other moms about the importance of friendship, the ineptitude of husbands, and the latest kidnapping schemes. I write. If the handyman visits, I click the watch off, clicking it on again only when my butt is back in the saddle. Sometimes I accumulate my writing time over six interruptions, clocking as little as fifteen minutes at a stretch. But I log it and stake my claim.

Some parents use a commute to separate their identities. I use my stopwatch. Click. I'm a writer—productive, efficient, meeting deadlines. Click. I'm a mommy—changing Jessica's dress for the fourth time because purple and green will not do. Click. It's writing time. However, the mommy appears at the keyboard instead, muddling over the morning shoe tantrum. Click. It's time for the preschool pickup. Yet as I jump into the car I'm as dejected as Cinderella at the ball, leaving the dance while the music is still playing. Often I just do a little bit of everything badly.

But on good days I call it balance. With my stopwatch, a line is established between the writer and the mother, a structure given to the otherwise undefined existence called Mommy Works at Home. (Am I a working mother, a stay-at-home? Let me check my watch.)

Atchity's technique has helped me put aside that chronic mommy complaint about not getting anything done. I see it on the stopwatch: two hours spent writing, that very morning, though later from the diaper changing table, it's hazy.

I do get a lot done. I just don't remember doing most of it.

Who says stuff can't change your life?

The Ideal Family

Be patient the first few times you eat together.
It is usually less than relaxing at first.

—JOAN LEONARD, *Twice Blessed*

When we're at home we always eat dinner with the boys. Heaven knows why. It will eventually give us ulcers, and even in my most optimistic moments I can't honestly believe that their childhood is being enriched by the warm and tender memory of those family meals accompanied by a steady stream of directives: "No, you can't make a sandwich with your potato chips. . . ."

—JEAN KERR, *Please Don't Eat the Daisies*

Six-thirty P.M. Perfect. The peas are tender in the pot, the pasta al dente. Jessica sits at the dining-room table in her high chair next to a pile of napkins. She's even wearing her bib.

With one small child I ad-libbed dinners. Somehow we all ate, but it wasn't much of an affair. Now we're a family of four, however, and Jessica is a toddler. It's time to launch that great tradition: the family dinner.

"Time to eat, everybody," I announce brightly from the kitchen.

No response.

"Dinner!" I pause. "Bill, can you please bring Isabelle?!"

Still no response. This always seems strange. After all, I can hear *them*. I try again. "Can you hear me?"

Pleas from Isabelle to her father for more playtime reverberate from her room. To serve or not to serve? This is the question. Jessica and I are hungry. I put the food on the plates. Ten minutes later, Bill and Isabelle have still not appeared.

My mother had a bell. I want a whip. Nothing gets cold faster than pasta. "DINNER!" I holler.

"*Whaaaa!*" cries Jessica, shaken by my yelling.

"We're coming!" shouts Bill.

A few minutes later, everybody sits down. Bill says grace. This is appropriate: getting a family with toddlers all seated together at the meltdown hour is truly a miracle. Isabelle is not hungry. Jessica, who is, has a logistical problem. She sees the peas. She can hold a fork. But she cannot coordinate them. Erupting in frustration, she beats the recalcitrant peas, sending them, along with flecks of pesto, flying—*splat*—onto Daddy's shirt.

Now, it always strikes me as odd, given the condition of, say, his office, that Bill hates getting his shirts stained. The tiniest splotch torments him. "Jessica!" he says sternly, dabbing a napkin and rubbing the stains.

I get a spoon. My little one throws it on the floor, screaming, "No!"

"Milk, please," says Isabelle.

"I'll get it," says my husband, trying to help.

"NO! I WANT MOMMY TO GET IT!" yells Isabelle.

"Never mind, Bill, I'll get it," I respond. My chair, after all, is closer to the kitchen.

Why is my chair closer to the kitchen?

Milk delivered, I sit down. Ah, finally—the magical moment of family unity. "So," I sigh, mustering a smile. "How was everybody's day?"

"Oops!" My firstborn spills her milk, splashing Daddy.

"Isabelle!" shouts Bill, now splattered with milk as well as pesto. I know what he is thinking: cooking is my job. Cleanup is his. Pesto? Why pesto? Pesto is greasy. Pesto is green.

Up for a rag for Bill. After mopping up the floor with it, he hands it back, dripping. No wonder my mother ate standing at the kitchen counter. Why sit down?

I take the rag back to the kitchen, return, and eat a second bite of cold pasta.

Bang, bang, bang, goes the fork on the high-chair table, attacking peas. Lowering his head, the man flecked with pesto and splotched with milk suddenly grabs a pile of mail from the center of the table. With an intensity usually reserved for critical academic analysis, Bill dives into his frequent-flyer statement.

"Mommy," cries Isabelle, "can I have cereal? PLEASE?!"

Five minutes lobbying for cold pasta and peas—a lost cause. It must have been slipping all that liver to the dog under the table growing up: I just can't get enthused about forced feeding. The parenting guides also fail to mention that delightful combination of a time-out given to a toddler suffering a blood-sugar low. So instead of giving one, or insisting on the green dinner, I cave in, fetching Cheerios. I also get paper towels: the frequent-flyer statement is now speckled with pesto. Go, baby, go!

Finally sitting, I feel the words forming like a great proclamation: I, Jennifer Hull, aka Mommy, do hereby resign as keeper of the family flame. But Bill is mouthing something that I can't hear, and Isabelle, who I can, has a question.

"Mommy," she asks, digging into her Cheerios with relish and flashing a charming toddler grin, "when can we go to Disney World?"

One reason I wanted a larger family was to do bigger things. Those of us who keep reproducing are nothing if not a little ambitious in the family way. The books and magazines are filled with cute little rituals and outings—meaningful family dinners, pumpkin-patch visits, and memorable vacations, to name but a few. The traditional wisdom is that families who cavort together stay together.

Yet early on, these ventures prove irrational at best, masochistic at worst. After a few tries it became clear: dining with toddlers is for morons. First, dinner coincides with what all experts agree is the kiddie meltdown hour. Second, all of us, and especially toddlers, are supposed to eat five or six small meals a day, not feast before bed. Third, full meals are wasteful and messy. Little kids' appetites are highly erratic, but they usually paw the food enough that it has to be thrown out. What doesn't go in the garbage often ends up on the floor. For at least one parent, and often two, the family dinner with toddlers is a lot of work.

Yet dinner is a no-brainer compared to that other great tradition: the family vacation. I started packing three days in advance: two sizes of diapers, wipes, food for four, sweaters, two changes of kids' clothes, Silly Putty, Play-Doh, coloring book, crayons, gum for ear popping—all this just for the plane. I posted a large note: DON'T FORGET BABY SLING—Bill's dour expression, upon my forgetting his favorite baby carrier on a prior vacation, forever seared in memory. I packed the suitcases, searching for the clothes the kids rarely use in Florida but will need in California, and made a sweater run. And Bill even managed to carry it all: two car seats, one stroller, one diaper bag, the cross-country survival kits, and one Portacrib.

We colored, we created, we ate our way from East Coast to West. We survived a marital argument at the rental-car counter, and when the car seats wouldn't fit, well, we unpacked one vehicle and got another. We stopped at the grocery store to buy breakfast food. We spook-proofed the rooms in the house we were staying at, plugged in the night-lights, and bathed the kids before bed. I made another grocery run in the morning. I even figured out how to use the microwave to warm Jessica's milk. And soon after, with a mommy-made picnic for four, we found ourselves on a gorgeous stretch of beach outside of San Diego, sun setting, the light just right, and two toddlers in my lap crying, "I don't want to eat with Daddy."

Ah, the family vacation with little ones! All those magical moments and meaningful conversations: "No, I didn't want you to come just to carry stuff. . . ." "Can you shake out the towels while I run the bath?" "But I thought *you* brought the buckets back." Not to mention the post-outing analysis: "I'm sure it will get easier as they get older." "Of course they love you!" "Well, at least I made sandwiches." It's so frustrating not to have fun when you've paid so much, so difficult to enjoy yourself when Cinderella gets left in the sand.

And sex? On vacation? With the big girl sleeping on the floor by the marital bed and the little one convinced her new quarters are haunted? Well, it happens, it does—just as some people climb Mount Kilimanjaro on holiday, and I dare say it might be a feat of nearly the same magnitude.

After a few difficult outings, I decided that a bigger family, at least initially, calls for smaller adventures. Older kids are one thing. They can find the bathroom. They may even remember the trip. More intrepid parents, of course, will not be stopped and will develop a host of survival techniques to keep them going. Yet my figuring, with two toddlers, was this: why schlepp little people who don't know Calcutta from California but need more luggage than Madonna to far-flung destinations for thousands of dollars when you can blow bubbles for ninety cents in your own backyard? I finally got it at Christmas, when the girls abandoned a dozen gifts to play with the packing popcorn. With small children, it's almost impossible, and pointless, to plan for fun.

So we decided to temporarily cut back, traveling less with two kids than we had with one. We limited our family outings and I lowered my expectations. Buying the Christmas tree became less a Kodak moment than a mission that may, or may not, go according to plan. More than with our first, we also started thinking kid-friendly. How far is the bathroom? How long is the walk? How loud can we be?

And finally, after watching my husband scrape squished peas off the floor, wall, and high chair for the umpteenth time, I bagged the family dinner. I felt guilty about this. The vision of our clan assembled around the dinner table is one I hold dear.

Then I read of another woman who abandoned the family dinner, deciding there were better opportunities for time together than the evening meltdown hour, and thought, *Right on!*

Six-thirty P.M. Perfect. Bill has just called from the park, having met Nancy there at five-thirty. The kids have played and eaten sandwiches and yogurt from the lunch box. Just back from the gym, I've got broccoli steaming on the stove for their return and am chowing down leftovers. It's a ten-minute dinner, but divinely serene. And by the time my little ones knock at the front door, I'm finished. It took me a while to figure it out. But the flight attendants' admonition, "For those of you who are traveling with small children, put on your oxygen mask first before assisting your child," also works well with eating.

Traditions seem like they should sparkle, at least come in pretty paper. Yet what else can I call it? The ritual, these days, is firmly established. Shoes off by the door. Shake out the sand.

Lunch box needs to be cleaned, but glory hallelujah—the crumbs all went on the ground. I offer broccoli to everybody and leftovers as well to Bill. Having worked up an appetite at the park, Isabelle scarfs down the vegetables. Jessica opts for warm milk. Serving himself, Bill happily eats reading his mail, pesto and milk free.

I look forward to someday dining with people who can clear the dishes and help set the table. I can't wait to explore the world more with my girls once the memory of diapering on the floor of a plane's hold recedes. The bit of vacation fun we've had has whetted my appetite for more.

However, the Brady Bunch kids were beyond vegetable tantrums when their family life was chronicled. If I postpone eating until everybody is assembled, I'll be the hungry martyr-mom. And if I make everyone sit through a meal, we'll miss the impromptu ballet show.

So I whirl around, on autopilot but with a full stomach, through my own kitchen; the great advantage of home is in knowing where things are and how the microwave works. We delight, as a family, in Isabelle's treasure from the park: a sparkly pink barrette.

It's not from Shakespeare, but it's the best advice for this stage of life: Keep it simple.

Choices

It is nothing short of a miracle every time
a woman with a child finishes a book.

—Erica Jong

Monday. Four P.M. Three weeks down. One to go. I am standing in the kitchen with Marta*, the baby-sitter substituting for Nancy, who is out of town. Bill and I are trying to get the kids to leave the house with Marta so we can work. Just a year old, Jessica is willing to go. But Isabelle, now three, is digging in her heels, a practice she's perfected over several long weeks.

Adding a child to the family ups the ante with baby-sitters. Depending on how many children you have, it can make it hard to find anyone to watch them. We got lucky with Nancy, who started working for us before Jessica's birth. Nancy is great with kids and loves babies in particular. Working out of the house, and speaking Spanish myself, I know her well, and our relationship is good. The kids love Nancy. So do I—and more every minute since she left town.

* *Not her real name.*

It's not entirely Marta's fault. She's a good soul and, like a substitute teacher, is in a tough role. In addition to being simpatico, Nancy and I have that eternal key to happiness with children that Marta and I lack: a routine. Over time we've developed a thousand little understandings about caring for the kids. Nancy's English is also better than Marta's, making it easier for her to communicate with Isabelle. Yet, in addition, though Marta is doing well tending Jessica in the mornings while Isabelle is at school, she simply does not have the right stuff for the difficult job of handling two toddlers later in the day.

And that, on this hot afternoon, makes two of us. For although my second child doesn't even talk yet, I can barely think straight for the din in the kitchen, much less manage the kids. My bilingual skills, usually such a blessing in Miami, have my head swirling.

Bill, ever rational, begins in measured English, "You should ask Marta to take the kids out. They need exercise."

Marta, responding in Spanish, after I suggest the idea, says, "Señora, it's too hot to take the kids out."

Bill, in English: "Jennifer, have you seen the baby sling?"

Me to husband: "Why do you want the sling? She doesn't know how to use the sling. . . . Bill, don't even think of taking them out yourself."

Bill, in English: "I just want to know where it went."

Isabelle, in full-bodied, toddler scream: "I won't go out!"

Marta, in Spanish: "Señora, by the way, you shouldn't give Jessica peas or corn. The skins could get caught in her intestines."

Me, in English: "Bill, they can just stay here. It's okay. I'll get them started playing in Isabelle's room. Why don't you go work?"

Writer to Mommy: "Why don't you?"

Marta, in Spanish, in the kitchen: "Señora, these paper towels are no good. You need to buy Bounty. Bounty doesn't fall apart when it gets wet. Sometimes by trying to save money you can waste money."

Mommy to Marta, in Spanish: "Forget the kitchen. Let's all go play in Isabelle's room. Then I'll go upstairs to work."

Writer to Mommy, later: "Thirty minutes in office listening to toddler tantrum does not a book make. If you're going to engage in García Márquez–like magical-realism dialogues, at least let me take notes."

And doesn't a hundred years of solitude sound divine right now?

I've wanted to write a book for years. However, each time I've tried, something has interfered. After Isabelle's birth, I put this goal aside. In the tumult of new motherhood, I was happy to stay in the writing game at all, my parenting articles and essays serving as a professional lifeline.

With my second child, however, motherhood seemed less like a short-term crisis than part of a life to which I would, as before, eventually have to answer. After years of birthing babies and tending little ones, I also became something I'd never expected: middle-aged. A young writer can put things off. A middle-aged writer feels the deadline in her bones. Six months after Jessica's birth, I posted an index card with the words "Write a book" above my desk.

But what to write about? I didn't want to do a book involving a lot of interviewing and reporting. I was already doing magazine articles, and with my second daughter starting to babble and a toddler interrogating me, I couldn't imagine spending more time on the phone. I opened my old files for a memoir about living in Nicaragua. Yet up to my ears in bath bubbles, that life seemed as accessible as a trip to the moon. The outline for a book on child-free women I started years ago felt a bit remote too. So what?

Then, about a month before Marta's arrival, I was giving Jessica a bath when it hit. Wrapping the baby in a towel, I ran to the kitchen counter and frantically began making notes. This time I had it: a clear theme, dramatic material, and that critical element earlier projects had lacked: a central character with skin as thick as a rhino's hide—my husband. Thus began my book on motherhood.

Now, with my first child I faced that great question: to work or not to work? Most women aren't fortunate enough to have this choice. I did, but didn't want to make it. And having heard about how much babies sleep, I didn't think I'd have to. However, a few sessions at the keyboard with a writhing infant, and dragging the whole family to my office so I could research a magazine article on deadline and still nurse, quickly dispelled the notion that baby and work could easily be combined. One child made it clear. Two made it indisputable: Caring for kids is a full-time job. You either do it yourself as a parent or are lucky enough to have Grandma available, pay for help, or use the TV. We are paying for someone to provide childcare—as Bill points out the next afternoon.

Ah, the joy of having a husband who works at home.

"You should get her to take them out or we'll never get any work done," says Bill. "Isabelle isn't used to being in the house this long. She's going crazy, and so am I."

Marta, in Spanish: "I'm happy to take them out."

Mother, in shock: "You are?"

"Sure," nods the baby-sitter.

Yes! I pack a lunch box in record time for Marta to take them on an afternoon walk. If they leave now, I'll have ninety minutes to write.

But the rebel commander has not been consulted in the talks.

Isabelle bursts into tears: "I am not going with *her*. I want to work in your office with *you.*"

Games. Books. Diversions. After all, it is hot—ninety degrees and Florida humidity making it feel well over one hundred. No decent mom would send the kids and baby-sitter out in this weather, even if Daddy has no such trepidations. "If you can just keep them away from the stairs that lead to my office, that would be great," I tell Marta in Spanish.

"Fine, Señora," she agrees.

Leaving Marta and the kids playing in Isabelle's room, I race up to my office, print a book chapter, and pull out a pen.

"No! No! No!" Nasty screams echo from the bottom of the stairs: the Mickey Mouse operation has moved. I look at the page again, something curdled and hot swirling inside me. *Scrrrapppeeee*. Isabelle drags her desk and places it at the bottom of the stairs. Calm coaxing words in Spanish. Defiant toddler English. *Plunk, plunk, plunk*. Jessica squeals in glee as dozens of crayons hit the floor like little drumsticks.

God, no wonder Sylvia Plath committed suicide: her kids were one and three.

"I want to play doctor," I hear Isabelle tell Marta in English. "Can you please get the doctor's kit?"

"Sure, I'll get the dolls for you," Marta responds in Spanish.

Chapter three. All telling. No showing. And remarkably like Vicki Iovine. Damn! Why does my writing always sound like the last author I read? Should I read at all? Am I just a copycat?

Pages of garbage. About being happier than ever before. About the velvety joys of baby flesh. A chapter title: "The Perfect Midlife Crisis." Who wrote this? What was she thinking? I circle a few decent phrases and cross out the rest.

Downstairs: Abracadabra! The toddlers have turned into baby alligators slamming their scaly tails against bookcases and tabletops. *Plop, plop, plop*. Jessica pulls the books from the shelf, squealing with delight at her new demolition skills.

Shit. Is Isabelle's penny collection on the low bookshelf or the high one? Will Jessica find it and swallow one?

Persistence. Writing is 90 percent persistence. The media speak of working and stay-at-home mothers, as if these identities were always separate and distinct, their divisions nice and neat. Especially after the second child, though, many women I know are doing something very messy in between, running businesses from the bedroom while someone else or a video occupies the kids part of the time. I put my earplugs in and return to chapter three. *Plop, plop, plop*, go the books.

Damn! The Day-Glo Walgreens earplugs may be cheap, but they don't work at all. Sometimes by trying to save money you can waste money. . . .

And I just know it. Marta will not see the pennies. Maybe the paper towels. Surely the peas. But not the pennies. I push my manuscript aside. The writer is no match for a mom with the emergency room on her mind.

Downstairs I find the penny collection on a high shelf, untouched. The girls are happy to see me, though.

A day later? Two days later? Two P.M. It's mommy time: I've structured my work schedule to spend midday with the kids, doing the school pickups, giving baths, reading stories, and starting naps—an arrangement that is usually pretty ideal. Marta is in the kitchen. Jessica continues her joyful exploration of our bookshelf. Inexplicably, in the last week, my snoozer has stopped napping.

One by one, my little girl hands me pieces of my past with a bright grin. I haven't looked at these books in years.

Outsmarting the Female Fat Cell. Hmmm. That fat cell's no dimwit; she's still hanging on despite a dozen diet books. Can Jessica have this? Yes, she can.

West with the Night by Beryl Markham, the great aviatrix, who was the first person to fly solo across the Atlantic from east to west. No diapers or wipes on that flight.

Cheap Sleeps in Paris. Oh God, anything but the book that guided Bill and me to that sweet pension on the Left Bank years ago!

Dejected, I put the travel book back on the shelf and step outside to get the mail. *Boom. Boom. Boom.* Three rejections in a row on my essays. I read Dr. Seuss to Jessica. "*Boom, boom, boom.* Mr. Brown makes thunder! He makes lightning! *Splatt, Splatt, Splatt.*" And it's very, very hard to get rejections like that.

Well, I can at least get my oldest down for a nap. One of motherhood's joys is that life is so full that when you bomb on one front you can usually succeed on another. Asking Marta to watch Jessica, I scoop Isabelle up and take her outside. My three year old quickly falls asleep on my shoulder as I rock her. Putting my nose in her hair, I inhale the fresh scent of baby shampoo. The pleasures of working at home with children, like the travails, are all tiny and fill the senses. My cup runneth over until, gazing over Isabelle's head, I notice something in the stroller.

What the hell is that light brown liquid in the baby bottle?

Later, I approach Marta.

"But Señora, it's *Diet* Coke," she protests.

"You're giving Jessica Coke?!" I exclaim in Spanish, turning to look at my wakeful baby.

"But Señora," says Marta, gravely, "she *likes* it."

Now, I know what a good mother would do in this situation because I am surrounded by them. Amy left her sales job to stay at home. Laura bagged accounting to raise her daughter. A good mother, of the stay-at-home sort, would boot the baby-sitter and do the job herself.

And the working moms employed outside the home? Well, these amazing paragons of productivity would simply do what they always do: the impossible, scouring the working-mommy network to find a new baby-sitter on short notice. Then they would return to their honorable task of supporting the family.

But I am neither of these. Instead, I am the worst kind of mom: one who works mainly for herself. My work is helpful but not essential to the family income. Worse, at the moment I am writing a book for which I don't have a contract and that my rejected essays indicate I lack talent for as well.

Yet unlike the mom who works outside the home and would see only the Diet Coke in the bottle, I've spent enough time elbow to elbow with Marta to see her good points. Marta is not my favorite baby-sitter. I would not hire her permanently. However, she's a God-fearing soul who is trying to pass on a little religion with the paper-towel advice. I feel Jessica is safe with her, and with only a week to go, it isn't worth finding a replacement. Nor does firing her seem fair. In addition, much as I hate to admit it, while Diet Coke might have been grounds for dismissal with baby number one, the bar is lower with the second.

And as for my husband? Well, he's just doing his thing, working during the day, helping get the girls to bed at night, hosing diarrhea off the Portacrib every morning. What more could a mom want?

But he's big. He's grown. He's there. And at nine on the evening after the Diet Coke discovery, he has just returned from his night *out.*

"Jennifer," Bill asks calmly, after the kids are in bed, "where are the sippy-cup tops? They're all missing."

That's it. I didn't sneeze my way through News 101 that horrible allergy-ridden fall in graduate school in Missouri for this. "YOU get to go out with your friends and have fun! YOU get to do what you want! I can't even leave the room without somebody screaming for me. I don't care about sippy-cup tops. I hate sippy cups." Making a fist, I smash the strawberries I've been cutting up, watching bits of red pulp splatter onto the floor. "YOU don't care about whether we buy Bounty! Why should I?"

I wash dishes violently as my husband sits, listening. "I don't want my life to be about paper towels and sippy cups. I want to write. We should have put the kids in daycare. I can't take it anymore. My girlfriends are working full-time, doing interesting things. What am I doing? I'm a big failure. I'm not even doing well with the kids. My book makes no sense; I can't even think straight. Working out of the house sucks: all I hear from my office is screaming. And I can't even be with Jessica because Isabelle is so demanding right now."

My husband blinks as I continue. "And I never get to talk to anybody who understands. My mom friends are all busy. Chris is on a deadline. Kathleen is consumed with moving. All the new mothers in the park talk about is burping and baby gas. I've never met such boring people in my life. I just want to get out of here."

I storm off to the bedroom, throw on a dress. I am going to drive down U.S. 1. I may even start smoking again. Driving. Smoking. It worked in high school.

Yet what's on U.S. 1? Toys"R"Us. Borders, with its row upon row of parenting books. And just what am I going to do? Drive, so I can tiredly drive back? Princess La Poo has had diarrhea for six weeks and will be up at dawn for the total body, clothes, and crib cleansing. Princess Yahoo is going to be ready for full combat by afternoon. And, if last night is any predictor, one or the other will be up at midnight needing cough syrup. I don't know why people criticize working mothers for not spending enough time with their kids when there are *twenty-four* hours in a day.

Beaten and bowed, I return to the kitchen.

"Are you ready to talk yet?" my husband says tiredly.

"Yes."

We walk to the bedroom.

"First," notes Bill, "you have no short-term memory. Last week you were telling me how great Marta is. Two weeks ago you had so many ideas for your book that you said you were being channeled. Just Sunday, you said you're happier than you've ever been."

Motherhood. The great mental eraser. I recall none of this.

My husband continues, his analytical mind dissecting the problem as neatly as a surgeon's knife. It's hot. Everybody's sick. Isabelle doesn't understand Marta well and doesn't like being indoors. Jessica, having just learned to walk, is especially demanding. These are passing problems, not a life.

But I'm a cacophony of conflicting selves. I'm thinking about *Cheap Sleeps in Paris* and that French pension that I shared with a man looking remarkably like the one talking. I'm thinking of Joan, who quit her finance job to stay home full-time and recently gave me a rundown on a host of kids' activities I'd never heard of around town. I'm thinking of Chris and the law conference that took her away for three days of adult conversation and two nights alone in a hotel.

That's it. A conference isn't doable, but I can take the kids to My Gym, a place Joan said has children's activities and air conditioning. This creative business is just a damn nuisance, anyway.

"Uh huh," says my husband. "I think we should have several plans."

Okay, plans I can accept. So we lay them out. First, the good-mommy scenario: I will take them to My Gym and leave Marta to do housework, of which there is always plenty. Then the working-mommy rain plan: I will print drafts of book chapters in the morning and edit at Borders in the afternoon, leaving the kids and Marta at home. Finally, the evil working-mommy, mean-employer deal: I will pack the lunch box and diaper bag ahead of time so that if Isabelle doesn't nap and can be persuaded to leave the house, Marta can stroll them in the afternoon.

It's complicated. However, my husband is a tax lawyer. He can play all angles.

Though, if the matter had been in his hands, he would have sent them out in the heat days ago.

The next afternoon arrives. It's sunny, humid, and ninety-three degrees.

I do not even consider going to My Gym. Instead I pack a lunch box, slather the kids in sunblock, bribe them, and send them out in the double stroller with Marta. Then I go up to my office, pull the drafts out of my purse, and start editing.

I feel guilty. I'm not Joan, whisking her children off to a fabulous kiddie event. I'm not Mary, the hardworking soul who earns half the family income and makes up for her absence during the week by spending every minute with the kids on weekends. High-flying fund manager Kate Reddy was a mommy missing in action in the novel *I Don't Know How She Does It*, but her poverty-ridden childhood and irresponsible, debt-laden dad justified it all in a sentence or two. And though the heat doesn't bother the kids, I hate sending Marta out in it.

Yet if I tried to fudge work-family issues with my first child, with two, choices must be made. Long ago, writing on a prescription pad, my father's psychiatrist made it clear: writers write.

It's only an hour. For a writer, though, one quiet hour can be worth three noisy ones. In silence, I feel something familiar emerging. I can read again. I can think. The page is clear. Working quickly, I kill cute chapter titles such as "The Perfect Midlife Crisis." I slash through poetic paragraphs that imply that I have motherhood figured out. I write now not from on high, but from the swamp, about alligators—tiny, treacherous, and oh-so-beloved. I bag my plan to write a bestseller in four months and aim for one productive hour, this afternoon.

When they return I have a draft of chapter three. It's jumbled, like a poorly hewn opening through dense Florida mangrove. I look much worse than in my previous version. But it's all true.

My children return with mangoes in their hands and smiles on their faces. They look like rosy-faced cherubs, not baby alligators at all, even as they splash wildly in the wading pool. Marta is red-faced from the heat but seems pleased to have finally gotten them out.

At night Bill reads books to the girls. I whip up a banana smoothie and make the Barbie toothbrush talk.

The next morning, while Jessica is at the park with Marta, a friend with grown children calls. "I admire how good you are with the kids. I feel somehow like I did it all wrong," says my friend, who had her children young and often expresses regret about how motherhood interfered with her writing ambitions.

I laugh. "I'm not always good. I get crazy when writing and the kids' needs clash. And I have help. I have all the advantages. Fathers are also much more involved these days than they were when you were raising kids," I explain. "Anyway, you were so young when you had children, and you were in such a difficult situation. You didn't have the choices that I do."

"Yes. By the time you had kids you were a fully formed person. I didn't even know who I was," sighs my writer friend.

A fully formed person. Battering strawberries. Threatening to drive off in the dark. Hiring a sitter who gives her baby Diet Coke.

I want to clarify. But it would take the whole morning to explain, if I could at all. And for the moment, I feel serene, something essential having been decided during the mango hour.

Anyway, I sense that my friend isn't really listening. Instead, it seems, she's thinking about choices: choices she made, choices she wishes she'd had, choices that were made for her—a long time ago.

Language Lessons

Then one day it happened. I had two children who talked.

In many ways it went as expected. The number of little "I love yous" increased. However, so did the noise level in our house. I've barely sat down in my kitchen since, for all the new verbal demands and requests.

What has surprised me, however, as Jessica has learned to talk and Isabelle has perfected her linguistic skills, are the language lessons I've gotten. Whole new expressions and phrases have entered my vocabulary. Others have acquired new meaning. William Safire wouldn't get it. But the following vocabulary primer may help moms survive the cacophony that follows their younger child's first words.

Of course the competition for Mom's attention begins long before both children can speak. Once the little one starts talking, however, the kids' requests seem to grow exponentially, one child's queries prompting the other to make her own. And now mobile, the younger one can track you down. This delirium of competing demands has given new meaning to many words and expressions, including:

You can't please all of the people all of the time, and its corollary, You can't be all things to all people. Yet how we moms try. In a classic case, I scoop up Isabelle for morning cuddles when she is four. We usually savor "cozy time" alone until her sleepier sister awakens. But hark! Jessica toddles in and wants to get in bed too. I try to cuddle them both. But it would take four arms to do it right; nobody is happy. So I take them to the kitchen for breakfast. Once there, Isabelle protests that I promised to cuddle her. (Correction on Miranda rights: Anything you say *will* be used against you.) Leaving Jessica with her cereal, I return for five minutes in bed with my older child. It feels like twenty: feeling abandoned, Jessica wails throughout. When I leave Isabelle for Jessica, big sister bursts into tears too.

All of the people? After a friend spent a weekend scrambling to care for her baby, read to her toddler, and help her preschooler on the computer, she found herself not only exhausted but unpopular in her own home. "By Sunday night, I've busted my tail—and they're all mad at me," she says. Sometimes, with a clan, you can't please anyone at all.

No-win situation. Jessica wants me to play dolls. Isabelle is pleading for a book. And which video to play? That's as volatile a choice as the borders for a Palestinian state. Since my youngest began to talk, I increasingly face no-win situations. The word "trade-off" has new resonance too.

Guilt. I used to view this as an avoidable emotion. After all, if you do the right thing, there's no reason to feel guilty, and I could usually satisfy one child's desires. Yet a doubling of requests for stories, love, and attention from small, very cute people with delectable skin has made guilt unavoidable. I mean, in fifteen years they'll be asking to drive the car to South Beach, not snuggle.

Get off it. Yet there are too many sweet smiles at home to purge guilt there. Instead, you have to listen to a mommy friend describe feeling guilty while watching her fly around her kitchen. Doing so made me recall this valuable phrase.

Whiplash. Neck condition I used to associate with auto accidents. Now makes me think of the kitchen.

Workout. Previously used for gym routine. Now describes Sunday afternoons at home. Bath to bed to kitchen to dining room; the wheels on the bus go round and round. As Jessica puts it after turning three, "You can just go back and forth." (Gee, thanks.) In the dining room I help Isabelle with crafts. In the living room I'm the mommy doll in a game with Jessica. Had I appreciated my dexterity in filling food orders, I would have worked at a restaurant rather than a car dealership at sixteen.

No need for the gym on Sundays.

Divided attention. I considered writing a chapter on this. Problem was, no revelations have come from doing, being, or getting two things at once. The spiritual approach, after all, is to focus on one thing at a time.

"But wait," says my guru husband, who went to church in the morning and a Buddhist ritual in the afternoon. "Some believe divided attention is the first step toward self-realization. Followers of the spiritual teacher George Gurdjieff say divided attention can be used to become aware of yourself within your environment, fostering self-awareness, or what they call 'self-remembering.'"

"Yeah, right," I respond, nodding vaguely.

Best to leave the esoteric stuff to Jacqueline Kramer, author of *Buddha Mom: The Path of Mindful Mothering* and the mother of one. A longtime Buddhist, Kramer presents parenting as a path for spiritual growth through surrendering control and practicing loving-kindness.

Remembering who I am while getting them what they want has so far eluded me.

Given this state of affairs, it's easy to imagine that the situation is hopeless. It's not. Two expressions in particular can guide a mom through the most conflicting kiddie demands:

Just say no. Oh, the dangers of waffling, when the oldest has a vocal ally! It's not surprising that Nancy Reagan had raised two kids by the time she coined this phrase for the war on drugs. I was never a Reaganite, but I now understand what shc was saying.

Taking turns. Brilliant solution to the no-win situation: once Jessica understood taking turns, my world changed. Come to think of it, a great idea for world peace. Peace "talks"? I'm now skeptical. In fact, the whole United Nations looks different to me now. And clearly Al Gore and George Bush shouldn't have had to take their case to the Supreme Court.

Meanwhile, our tower of babble has elevated some words and phrases and demoted others, among them:

Thank you, Mommy. Music to my ears.

Please, Mommy. It depends.

Dinner time! Are they words if nobody ever hears them? The kiddie definition of this command seems to be "Go play!" and even Bill is incredibly slow to come to the table.

And some words and expressions that have been allies to me as a journalist have become foes:

Why? Now that I'm so often on the other side of this question, it sounds different. No wonder politicians get squirmy at press conferences. Repeated over and over by more than one person, "why" feels abusive.

The other day, for instance, Isabelle asked, "Why do people get chapped lips?" I provided a long, detailed explanation about dry lips. As soon as I finished, Jessica asked the same question. It's been three days now, and I've described chapped lips twenty times. And I swear, I'm not hiding a thing.

Why not? Worse.

There are no dumb questions, only dumb answers. A colleague at the *Wall Street Journal* passed this nugget along to help me sort out confusing financial statements with verbally challenged CEOs. Now it sounds a lot different. There definitely are dumb questions.

Then there are those strange things that come out of my own mouth these days as a result of our newfound cacophony:

That's my name. Don't wear it out. Yuk! Am I really saying this? My own mother didn't even say this.

Swivelhead. You don't know the story? A mom's head swivels around so much while she's responding to her kids' requests that it flies off and has to be put back on. "Really?!" says Isabelle, awed. Great mommy morality tale by yours truly. Miraculously, it reduced requests for one whole day.

And finally, some expressions that ring truer than ever now that my younger child has found her voice:

Silence is golden. Absolutely.

You can't please everyone, so you have to please yourself. There may be hope after all. For if I haven't gotten to "self-remembering" from divided attention, when my kids' words pull me different directions, this phrase gets me through.

The Expert

The father with the two young boys at Borders is as big as a football player but looks as though he is about to collapse.

Many men say the second child really makes them a dad; I sense one being formed before my eyes. It looks like it could be this fellow's first solo Saturday outing with the kids. "How's it going?" I ask.

"Oh, God, my wife's at a conference for the weekend," he sighs, looking at his watch. "I can't believe it's only one in the afternoon. I'm not sure what we're going to do. We already hit Burger King."

"Yeah, it's hard to find things to do with the kids when it's hot," I remark. "How old are your children?"

"Two and four," he responds.

"Why don't you take them to the car wash?"

"The car wash?" he asks.

"Yeah, the purple car wash on U.S. 1 is great. They've got free popcorn, and you can watch the car get sprayed with bubbles through these big windows. There's great sixties music too." I turn to Isabelle and Jessica. "What do you think of the car wash?"

"We love the car wash!" they chant in unison.

"Hmmm," he mumbles as the youngest boy jumps up and down pleading for a stuffed snake. "No," says the dad, looking down. "I don't want to buy a toy. We can buy a book."

Want. Major waffling. Definitely in need of help. "If you get here earlier you can catch Grasshopper Green—he's this funny old guy who reads stories," I note. "And you can bring a lunch and eat here."

"Yeah, I'm not sure Burger King was a good idea." Something happened at Burger King. I don't ask.

"But story time at Books and Books is even better because the bathroom is right off the children's section, and you can order a sandwich at the café."

"Really?" he pauses. "And where did you say the car wash is?"

"Bird and U.S. 1. It's the one with the big purple sign."

"Oh yeah, right. Thanks," he says, looking like he wishes he'd met me five hours ago.

"Anytime."

I first noticed it at Borders because the leap was so large. Motherhood's achievements are hard to measure, but this milestone was unmistakable; a few years earlier, I'd been the lost and frazzled parent in the same spot. Now, I was handing out advice to a muscle man and having fun with my kids as well.

Still, if the Borders dad confirmed it, the change in mommy consciousness had been underway for a while. A year after Jessica's birth, I became a parenting know-it-all, giving advice to all who asked, and many who didn't. Somehow I just couldn't help myself. One kid is a trial run. Two is a scientific sample. Whenever a parent looks even slightly in need of help, I run to the rescue.

Pregnant with Isabelle, I grew tired of advice givers. Now I find myself on the other side. Around new moms, in particular, I can barely stop talking. I don't think my friend Valerie, pregnant with her first, expected a full hour-long birth lecture for lunch. But she got it, despite my suspicious credentials as a two-time C-section gal. And, occasionally, even experienced parents like this dad get me going. If it takes two to break in some fathers, by the second child, most moms could write a parenting manual.

Giving advice is a sign of confidence. Pregnant with my second, I never expected to have so much. When my friend Kathleen, who has two older children, calmly advised me on what to expect with a second, I couldn't imagine being in her place. I rarely felt that assured with my first, my confidence as shaky as Isabelle's latest sleep patterns and my knowledge limited to one unpredictable toddler. Now, with two, I'm giving little parenting lectures. By Sunday night, the Borders dad will probably get there too.

Yet, like other veteran parents, I'm a strange mix of mother superior and fallen angel. Any theory that has survived both kids, I preach with the zeal of a minister. Having gotten two children to sleep through the night with the Ferber technique, it's more a faith than a strategy. However, my growing family has also taught me how little I can control, and my standards have fallen. Many new moms' questions, in particular, seem silly—the precise time to start potty training? Don't ask me.

Meanwhile, many "real" experts have fallen off of their pedestals, my experience with two kids having disproved a host of parenting adages, including "You will lose weight nursing," "These are the best years," and "You'll be ready for sex in six weeks." When life ran contrary to expectation with one child, I thought I was abnormal. Two has made it clear: a lot of parenting advice falls flat.

With my first, William Sears's baby sling proved a marriage saver, Daddy's indispensable tool. The pediatrician's "attachment parenting" approach also felt warm and fuzzy. But being tethered to two is another matter. You say, how many in the bed? The theory that sounded so cozy with one conjures up images of the chiropractor and sleep deprivation with two.

As I learned early on, while trying to enforce a toddler time-out with a baby on my hip, much of the experts' advice works a lot better in one-child families. The admonition to listen to your little one is a good one. But how, when the other is also talking? And can you really be heard with that calm voice all the experts prescribe amidst the din of two or more? Spending time alone with one daughter would be delightful—if it didn't make the other bonkers. As a child psychiatrist quoted in *Three Shoes, One Sock & No Hairbrush* put it: "Most childcare experts write as if a mother is only dealing with one child at a time when, of course, that is not usually the case."

I still consult the parenting guides. But my real advisors these days are other mothers who have been in the game long enough to have developed their own expertise. And as for older moms, like my own, who raised more than two? I'm on my knees. If you could just recount what you did instead of saying "You do what you have to do," it would really help.

Mostly, though, since Jessica's birth, I've relied on my own instincts. After a year of nursing, for instance, I simply stopped. I didn't read about it. I didn't call the La Leche League. One day I just quit. "Are you sure you don't want me to research this?" asked my professor husband. "No," I answered, rejecting the offer, free database access and all.

Two children have brought me to the most basic of parenting guides and the best-priced one too, my own common sense. For if with one I scrambled to gather information, I now know something else: expertise sometimes also means putting advice aside.

It's another warm spring day. Hands on her hips, the swim teacher stands by our pool. Her pupil huddles, crying, under Daddy's desk.

She has all the right credentials, but if she introduced herself to my firstborn, I didn't hear it, and her authoritarian style isn't working. Despite the instructor's firm grip, Isabelle quickly wiggled free and ran off. Twenty minutes of the lesson are spent coaxing her back into the pool, where there are no games, few pleasantries, and a lot of commands. "I'll call you if I want to schedule another lesson," I say later, knowing full well that I won't.

I wouldn't have been so decisive as a new mother. Swimming is a big deal in Florida, where many apartment buildings and houses have pools. And with all the articles on babies swimming underwater and toddlers diving like dolphins, the pressure is on. At four, Isabelle lacks the swim skills of many of her friends.

But as a mother of two, I'm confident about my decision. From her first bath, Isabelle has never enjoyed water. She only waded in the pool as a toddler after major cajoling on my part. Coming from a family of strong swimmers, I was initially confused by this. Yet Bill's people are catlike: the family joke each summer is about getting Daddy in the water. When Jessica cooed in her baby bath and lunged into the pool as a toddler, the genetic connection was confirmed. One daughter loved water and the other hated it.

My own mother stills swims for several hours a day, and I've always enjoyed it as well. With Isabelle, I want to pass on not just skills, but also a mommy-daughter love of the water. This won't happen under Daddy's desk.

So I fire the swim teacher and assume her duties. Still, I worry because Isabelle's progress is slow. Naturally cautious, she takes one dip at a time. While friends and little sister jump wildly into the pool, Isabelle slips in slowly, holding on to the side.

Then one day, when I'm fishing Jessica out after she dive-bombs into the water, my big girl yells, "Mommy! Watch! I can swim across the pool by myself!"

The pool is tiny, but it's a major step. Soon after, Isabelle begins swimming underwater. By five, she has an impressive backstroke and some breaststroke, too.

We surely would have made faster progress with a better teacher. Watching her splash happily and paddle away, however, I feel vindicated.

I may not be a certified swim instructor, but I'm an expert on my kids.

Missing the Baby-Doll Gene

At seven-thirty in the evening, five baby dolls lie neatly on the floor, towels serving as a blanket for each. I've only just begun to get their mother and her big sister ready for bed. Gee, it's hard to live with a mom who is better than you are.

Around the time I was pondering the genetic connection to swimming, my second daughter displayed a trait that made me marvel: Jessica, from the start, was a natural-born mom. It began with one baby doll. Then she had twins. Jenny and Patty look alike to everyone else, but like a true mother, Jessica sorts them out every time. These were followed by Katherine, Megan, and Mary, all of whom, like the others, not only get to bed on time but wear bibs too—something I swore to enforce with their mother after failing with her sister, to no avail.

Jessica's interest in baby dolls shouldn't have surprised me. Girls, after all, are supposed to like dolls. Yet Isabelle's dolls had been orphaned early: by Jessica's birth, both grandmas were under orders to send no more. Like many parents, I'd imagined a second child like my first.

However, one of the delights of a multichild family is seeing how different kids are from the start. Without a sibling for comparison, it was hard to appreciate Isabelle's unique attributes. When she swayed on the beat at five months, I figured that all babies have rhythm. When she refused to sleep, I assumed other moms were putting cereal in the formula. And when my first daughter abandoned her dolls, I wasn't surprised. I'd never liked them myself.

Then I got a girl whose feet barely left the ground, who slept like a rock, and who was the perfect mom. Noticing these qualities helped me appreciate Isabelle's unique attributes. With a big sister to compare her to, Jessica's special traits emerged quickly too. "She sings," I exclaimed to Bill one day. "She sings!"

The genetic connection also proved a relief. Having a second child who didn't climb counters, leap through the house like a gazelle, or fight sleep made me realize that Isabelle's curiosity and energy are wonderful qualities, but they'd definitely made her a demanding toddler and baby. Until Jessica's arrival I'd figured that I was just inept, my sample of one making it difficult to see that some kids are simply harder than others. Meanwhile, Jessica's proclivities justified some of my own. Her early inability to run explained my years of ditching track and field. Her passion for ice cream excused my Häagen-Dazs excesses. "Sometimes I worry about how much she eats," Nancy remarked gravely, after Jessica discovered solids. Not me. Like most parents I secretly delight in seeing my genes passed on, warts and all.

Writing an article on gender and kids, I learned that aside from the basic biological differences, many of the alleged male and female traits occur on a continuum, with girly girls on one end, boyish boys on the other, and many kids, as well as adults, in between. This, and Jessica's remarkable nurturing skills, convinced me that there's a baby-doll gene: women on the far end of the female spectrum have it. Those edging toward the male pole don't. My little theory proved helpful, explaining why one daughter loved baby dolls while the other preferred bouncing balls. Yet it also begged a question: if you lack the baby-doll gene, can you still be a good mom?

We're sitting in the living room with our friend Robin, who is pregnant with her second child and has a toddler. "Wow, Jessica is so good with her dolls," says my friend, watching our younger daughter tend Jenny and Patty.

"Yeah, Jessica is a better mom than Jennifer is," my husband laughs.

Excuse me!? Two C-sections; years of breast-feeding; a thousand witty imitations of Mickey Mouse, Donald Duck, and Mary Poppins—British accent and all—for this?

"Bill!" I exclaim, shooting my husband the evil eye.

Only a man could make such a direct hit on a mommy's heart so casually. "I think you're a great mom. You're just not a *natural* mom," Bill responds, nonplussed, explaining to Robin how I'd never been interested in small children before having my own.

Now is there anything more embarrassing than having your husband question your mothering in front of a woman you've been advising on the matter? I wanted to kill Bill, until I noticed our guest. Her face had relaxed, a smile emerged. She was the picture of relief. And despite the assault to my credentials, her questions continued. At age two, her daughter was mobile. Would she still need a double stroller when her second child arrived? Yes. Could we come to her house next time? Absolutely.

Hmmm . . .

I was pondering Bill's comment and my friend's reaction in the weeks that followed when a strange thing started to happen: "unnatural" moms started popping up everywhere. All had more than one kid and were better parents than they claimed. "I'm just not a natural mom," lamented a writer friend, later smothering her toddler with kisses and adding, "Isn't he delectable?"

"I don't know how I did it. I wasn't a natural mother," noted an older friend not long after, shaking her head in wonderment at how she'd raised four. "But they all turned out to be interesting, well-adjusted adults, which is no small accomplishment in this day and age." No kidding.

And from Katharine Graham, in her Pulitzer Prize–winning autobiography *Personal History*: "I never learned to be truly at ease with small babies, although I got better with each one." Presumably a lot better. Like my older friend, Graham raised four solid citizens.

Since then I've met and read of many more unnatural moms—so many, in fact, that I've come to wonder if Jessica's traits aren't an anomaly. The picture of the perfect mom—part Virgin Mary, part June Cleaver—endures. However, it's hard to find her at the park or in the memoirs. These unnatural moms and their kids have confirmed what I would have heard if I'd listened to Bill's comment instead of being defensive: an unnatural mom can still be a great one, even as family demands increase. In *I'm Okay, You're a Brat!*, Susan Jeffers describes what she calls "Loving-Being-a-Parent genes" but says that while they're helpful, they aren't essential. Writes Jeffers, who lacked the baby-doll gene herself but wrote the book with support from her grown son, with whom she's obviously close: "You don't have to love parenthood to be a good parent."

If Bill's calling me an unnatural mom bothered me at first, his claim that I'm a great mom also rings true. I'm not society's image of the perfect mom. Necessity is the mother of invention, however, and parenting is a learned skill too. I couldn't have imagined her during my child-free days, but the woman who can Band-Aid two boo-boos at a time, and do crafts in one room while feeding baby dolls in another, is one I now intimately know. And if I don't always enjoy the tasks involved, I love being a mom.

With time, I've also come to appreciate my unnatural-mom self, even found her a sanity saver. For if I initially worried about being a good mother without the baby-doll gene, I've learned that this is not the real issue. The call to motherhood is fierce and primary, and love for one's children will turn even the biggest bungler into a multitasking marvel. The challenge, especially as demands grow, is to be a happy mom. It's the unnatural mom who says no to special meal orders; refuses to dash to Toys"R"Us on Christmas Eve to fill last-minute requests; and insists, "Mommy needs some quiet time now too."

When my fingers are all thumbs doing ponytails, I try to remember that I can't pirouette either, but I taught my big girl to swim. Mothering a clan involves so many different skills that you can usually excel at something, and love isn't a matter of getting the kids perfectly scrubbed. Although more challenging with motherhood, it's still good advice: To thine own self be true.

Jessica's not likely to identify with my experience as a mom. Only two girls to put to bed and they're not under their blankies by seven-thirty?

But genes often skip a generation: my own mother tucked in a lot of baby dolls as a kid too. Though Jessica won't need the tips, this book may help her fathom a daughter or two.

Sharing a Room

Having more children often raises the issue of sharing a room. While common, this arrangement isn't ideal. Sharing a room can fuel rivalry and compound sleep problems, such as different nap times. Late-night conversations leave both parties restless. And by day's end, the chatty person can drive the quiet one nuts.

For these reasons, after Jessica arrived, my husband and I started sleeping apart.

Our kids *do* share a room, and they have all of the problems noted above. We would have separated them, but our third bedroom, my office upstairs, is too remote for a small child.

With a guest bed, however, it's perfect for an adult. And so, about a year ago, sleep deprived and each seeking refuge, Bill and I started alternating nights upstairs.

I never expected to do this. In my own family, adults sleeping apart always led to divorce. Before kids, I left the marital bed only when mad. The bed upstairs was previously reserved for guests.

But that was before little people claimed every inch of my body and all of my toiletries; before the nighttime wake-ups doubled; and back, before two, in that bygone era when sleeping together led to sex. In the past, I had only one princess strutting into the bedroom making grand pee-pee proclamations at midnight. As mommy protagonist Kate Reddy put it in *I Don't Know How She Does It*, "When I was younger I wanted to go to bed with other people; now that I have two children my fiercest desire is to go to bed with myself for a whole twelve hours."

Many couples don't have the space to sleep apart or wouldn't want to if they could. Some children wouldn't do well sharing a room, and brothers and sisters eventually must be separated anyway.

Yet our arrangement is no stranger than others I've encountered in that sleep deprived and cramped territory beyond one. After their second child arrived, one couple I read of turned their bedroom into a playroom, sleeping in a loft. A few generations ago, Shirley Jackson wrote of playing musical beds one night with her husband and three children due to colds and kids' wake-ups; by morning Jackson herself had changed beds five times. An eight-year-old girl I know complains that her situation is unfair because, unlike everyone else in her family, she doesn't *get to* share a room. Each night she climbs into her younger brothers' bunk bed. Finally, I recently heard of sisters, ages three and fourteen, who room together because their parents can't move the computers from the other available room. Having spent two weeks with the wires under my desk trying to connect to the Internet, I understand.

It's not clear how long our current arrangement will last. Bounding out of bed, Isabelle is a lark, while her sister needs to be pried out. They may not be compatible for long. When both stop waking us, the marital bed may look a lot more attractive.

Yet however long it lasts, I'm glad for our odd arrangement, because it's provided a valuable lesson: with a growing family, it pays to think unconventionally about space.

Jessica's birth put us beyond politically correct sleeping arrangements. Our debates over sleeping with baby Isabelle looked ludicrous. We now knew that the name of the game was to sleep—wherever, with whomever, and without concern for appearances. While my mother had purchased a lovely white crib with a pink-striped bumper for Isabelle, we put Jessica in a Portacrib in the bathroom off our bedroom. It wasn't cute or cozy, but she was the second child and slept well there, so we didn't care.

Bill and I slept together until Jessica was born. Then, after her birth, he moved upstairs. I nursed the baby in our bedroom during the night. He slept through and got Isabelle ready for school. I dealt with midnight colic. He handled get-ready-for-school tantrums. Square deal.

Then Jessica stopped nursing, and one night Bill moved back downstairs.

Together after a year apart! Two kids have dispelled any romantic fantasies: our bed, after a day with little ones, is now associated almost exclusively with slumber. But on this evening an essential piece of marital life has been reclaimed. After rejoicing at being together, my husband drifts off.

Then it begins. "*HurRRRGGGHHH, PPHHeeewww. HurRRRGGGHHH, PPHHeeewww . . .*"

Bill's snoring never bothered me much when it was one of the only sleep interruptions. Now, with a baby and toddler waking us, it feels cruel. I jostle him and hold his nose, a tactic that sometimes works. When neither stops the snoring, I wake him up. Given the premium on shut-eye, Bill sees this as a criminal offense. Unlike me, my husband has trouble falling back to sleep. For the next two hours, he's up, awoken not by the kids but his wife.

Night number two.

Okay, it would have been better if we hadn't started the philosophical conversation about the meaning of life at ten, but we hadn't had a good talk in two days, and a lot has happened. And we were further delayed by Isabelle, who stumbled into our room, half awake, at eleven. We're definitely behind as I settle into bed.

"What are you doing?" asks my husband, lights finally out.

"I'm getting comfortable," I respond defensively. Sleeping with someone who couldn't speak definitely had advantages. And did Bill's feet always stick out so much, pulling the sheets off the end of the bed?

"How many pillows do you have?" he continues.

"Three."

"Are you going to keep moving them around?"

"I'm just getting comfortable!" Damn, I'd almost forgotten: Bill sleeps like a corpse. Movement makes it hard for my husband to fall asleep and wakes him up. Yet each pregnancy has added a pillow to my sleep routine. One goes under my head, two under my legs. All three need to be rearranged in the middle of the night. And I don't know if it's from pregnancy or waking with babies—I now go to the bathroom at least twice a night, then fall straight back to sleep. By two A.M. my excursions are driving my husband crazy.

Night number three.

What looked like a martial achievement is beginning to feel like cause for divorce. I adjust my pillows in advance and use earplugs to block out the snoring. But after Jessica wakes us both at midnight, Bill turns to me bleary-eyed and asks, "Would you mind if I go upstairs?"

Since having kids, sleep has become the currency of our marriage, the gift we give each other. Seeing how tired my husband is, I urge him to go. The following evening, we switch beds.

At first it seems like another marital concession to motherhood.

Then, on a full night's rest, I get the report: Jessica was up at twelve for a diaper change. Isabelle climbed under the covers with Daddy at six.

Except for traveling and nights when we've had visitors, I haven't slept with my husband since.

"Are you sure she doesn't fit?" Bill asks a year later as we stand in our bathroom, looking at the Portacrib.

"Bill! Jessica's almost two!" I exclaim. "We'll stunt her growth if we don't move her."

Looking glum, my husband concedes that the Portacrib has become tight. The moment of truth has arrived. It's time to move Jessica into the bigger crib in Isabelle's room.

We brace ourselves for disaster. Now four, Isabelle rises earlier than her sister and seems certain to wake her up. It's also hard to imagine one's sleeping through the other's nighttime wakings. Some of the second-child books advise separating children, if possible, noting that kids need privacy and time alone. My parents must have agreed. I didn't share a room growing up, and when we moved, they quickly plastered over a small door connecting Jon's room to mine. Isabelle's excitement only fuels our anxiety. "Tonight? We're going to sleep together tonight?" she asks, jumping up and down.

It's Bill's turn on night duty. After putting them to bed—five times—I wish him luck and tiptoe upstairs. I'm prepared for a good, solid argument the next morning about Jessica's height, maybe even some measuring, when my husband greets me, smiling.

"They slept through," he says, looking surprised. "Isabelle woke up early, but says she let Jessica sleep more before climbing in her crib. She seems to have entertained her—I got up later than usual."

We burst out laughing. Our kids have done better sharing a room than we have.

A year later, Isabelle and Jessica remain good roommates, especially compared to the adults in the house. They squabble, but they don't go to sleep mad. They tolerate each other's disruptions much better than we do. Once Isabelle is snoozing, it's amazing what she can sleep through—Jessica's diaper changes, potty runs, and requests for toys don't disturb her.

Their conversations about Cinderella and the prince are infinitely more interesting than ours about the plumber. While there's sometimes major monkey business after the lights go out, they still fall asleep faster than Bill and I did, probably because they talk to each other more during the day. And Isabelle wouldn't even think of asking Jessica about the price of hurricane shutters in the dark.

Not that it's easy. I have to make an extra effort now to give my older girl privacy when she requests it—letting her listen to music alone in our room, for instance. Their evening antics sometimes drive me so crazy that I want not just to separate them, but to lock them up. Lately, sharing a room has also made the little one's nap a no-win. Eliminate it and she's cranky. Put her down in the afternoon and she torments big sister at night. From the kitchen, I hear them, after the lights are out.

"Isssaaabbbaaayyyuuulll! Please tell me a story!"

"No, Jessica! I'm tired!"

"Please!"

"Mommy! Jessica is in my bed!"

Other times big sister is the culprit. A few months before nursery school began, Isabelle announced, in the dark, that Jessica was to start school the next day. "But don't worry, it's fun," added big sister, slyly. Panicked, Jessica ran sobbing into the kitchen.

Yet mostly, our problems are their delight. Even during our worst put-downs, I can't help but notice: my children are having a blast. Overall, like many kids who room together, our girls love it, and can't wait for that next great adventure: bunk beds. Separating our kids now would almost be a punishment.

And on the mornings I find them "reading" together in bed, I wonder if I could.

Jessica, our director of human relations, likes to keep track of her people.

"Who's sleeping downstairs?" she asks one recent evening.

"Daddy," I answer.

"Who's sleeping upstairs?" she continues.

"Mommy."

"Where is Jenny?"

Hmmm. This is harder. While our whereabouts are predictable, Jessica's doll likes to hide.

At three and five, our girls are used to our unconventional arrangement. They know that the parent who sleeps downstairs will comfort them at night, get Isabelle ready for school, and give a major time-out if they wake the parent upstairs. They also know that the parent in charge is likely to be groggier than the one who appears, brightly, from Mommy's office.

This evening, it's my turn upstairs. I'm looking forward to feeling brighter because I'm not too sparkly now. The double dental appointment took some cajoling, the one P.M. time slot fitting into my work schedule but coinciding with the kids' afternoon slump.

Still, when Jessica bounds off, refusing to brush her teeth, I don't yell. I don't need to. The promised land is in sight. Turning off the lights, I tuck them in and tell them each something I'm proud of, a little mommy ritual that makes us all feel good. Isabelle beams upon being thanked for her cooperation at the dentist's office, then gives me her signature supersmack. Jessica says, "Tell me what you powd of," and grins as I congratulate her on finishing dinner. Then she pulls her blankie close and opens a book.

This is the latest bedtime strategy: Isabelle has to go to sleep. But having napped, Jessica can look at books in bed by the hall light, as long as she doesn't bother big sister. Tonight it works. Isabelle drifts off. Jessica flips some pages, then falls asleep too. All quiet on the kiddie front, I approach Bill.

Now, at least when Jessica and Isabelle keep each other up, they can enjoy it, blissfully ignorant of the price they'll pay for their nocturnal antics. In contrast, Bill and I face the conflict of wanting to connect at the end of the day but knowing we should hit the hay, an issue that no sleep arrangement can solve. Once we started sleeping apart, I started a ritual to preserve intimacy, lighting a bedroom candle and spending time with him there before we split up. However, having a great late-night conversation—or, God forbid, sex—is a mixed blessing when you're on the Princess La Pee and nightmare shift.

Tonight I light a candle but keep it short. We laugh about the dental appointment, agree that our little charges are the best and brightest, if exhausting, and decide that since I did the dentist, Bill will do the doctor. Then I pass the baton. As I head upstairs a little voice echoes down the hall. "Daaaaaddddyyyy, I have to go pooooo-poooooo. . . ."

Hearing Bill respond, I keep climbing. Upstairs, my office is as I left it, a fact that seems remarkable given the state of the rest of the house. The peach walls are free of scribble. Pictures of my parents, my brothers, and the kids are neatly displayed. By the bed, Edna St. Vincent Millay's biography sits waiting for a ten-minute read. The closet is jammed with rainy-day toys and birthday party decorations. But there are no Cinderella shoes on the floor, no duckies in the bath. I've got enough toiletries to shower and extra melatonin. If I wake in the middle of the night, it's no one's fault but my own.

It's not much extra sleep time—about fifteen minutes in the evening and morning. However, upstairs I'm safe from the kids' nighttime wake-ups and able to rise on my own. No six A.M. request for a story. No bouncy big girl using my bed as a trampoline. And I can pee and rearrange my pillows to my heart's content.

In the morning, Jessica wails for her blankie. Isabelle wants more cereal. The *beep-beep* of the microwave tells me that Bill is on duty. I need not respond.

It's a brief respite. But for a few minutes, every other morning, I awake in a room of my own—alone, unreachable, free.

And because of that, downstairs, I'm all theirs.

Lipstick Therapy

Crying. Clawing. Jessica and Isabelle are fighting over a rosy shade of Elizabeth Arden. The lipstick is losing.

I'm running that gauntlet called trying to get ready to go out to dinner with my husband and amuse the kids, who are rejecting him, at the same time. The makeup is the biggest hurdle. I've made popcorn as a distraction, but it sits on the bathroom floor untouched—no match for Elizabeth Arden and her buddies, especially when little sister gets to the makeup first. It's the sibling effect: Isabelle wasn't even interested in the lipstick until Jessica found it. Now nothing else will do. With one daughter, handing over the lipstick pacified. With two it sparks a war.

"Mine!" says Jessica, grabbing the gold-cased tube.

"No, mine!" Isabelle shouts back.

Maybe it's time to see that therapist again, the one who got me into this in the first place. She'll be surprised to learn that I have not only one, but two kids. However, I'll set her straight, telling her how much I love my girls and how well they're turning out—eating broccoli and reading books instead of watching TV. Then I'll talk about the violent feelings I have when they mutilate my Rich & Rosy.

And the lipstick thing, she'll ask, how did it start?

Oh, that magical afternoon, when Isabelle painted Jessica's toenails in Russian Red and I took pictures! "Look, Mommy, I even did my legs," my firstborn exclaimed.

A crash brings my attention back to the bathroom. Jessica has thrown the entire makeup bag at Isabelle. Whipping the brush through my wet hair and quickly pulling it back in a clip, I order my two and four year old to share. I long ago gave up on my hair and don't partake of the other mommy sanity savers: manicures, wine, sitcoms, serial shopping. But lipstick . . .

And you're a feminist? The therapist would ask.

Decked in Rich & Rosy, Jessica is marching toward the light blue bedroom rug. We're vacationing at a house shared with others. I can hear it now—the lipstick-on-the-rug call.

Adrenaline racing, I grab Jessica and carry her into an adjoining room. There, on a shelf, my mother appears in a picture with my brother, then a toddler, on her hip. She wears a beautiful scoop-necked dress. The red headband in her dark hair matches the vibrant shade on her lips. Next to her, I stand, about six years old.

How, I wonder, did she get those lips painted for that picture and all the others like it? She cared for two kids full-time, in an era when men didn't help. Yet in my memory her lipsticks stand full-bodied, glossy, and proud—not decapitated and flecked with bits of contrasting color from their comrades. I recall them lying neatly in her dresser drawer: Coral, Pink Bubblegum, Tangerine.

Ah, but the therapist would say, we can save that for next week.

Forget it! I don't need to pay $100 an hour to excavate my memories of watching Bugs Bunny and the Flintstones as a kid. When am I going to get it? Every couple has their parenting point of pride. The no-TV policy is ours. Were I on full-time with my children, I would have used it as a sanity saver. But since we have help, when the kids are around, we keep it off.

Yet pride cometh before a fall. You can't dress with one child climbing on the bathroom counter and the other threatening to paint the house rosy red. My vaunted first-time-mom standards have to go. If being a happy parent counts toward being a good one, second-rate may be more than sufficient. Who likes supermom, anyway?

Sweeping up Jessica and Isabelle, I plop them in front of the TV.

Bill's brow furrows. My husband thinks the boob tube turns kids' brains to mush and makes them rabid consumers. I agree. But they're headed for the Elizabeth Arden counter anyway. And he can't understand the depth of the fury unleashed as each of us females seeks to claim the Rich & Rosy and be the big girl.

For ten whole minutes, until the sitter comes, it's quiet. My lipstick is a sliver of its former self. It goes on fine with a brush though, despite specks of watercolor in the bristles. As I dab my lips, the scream retreats.

It's a daring act, applying Rich & Rosy around the corner from the lipstick thieves instead of in the car, a different feeling leaving the house a finished woman. The great advantage to not watching much television, though, is that, once on, it pacifies completely.

Lipstick Therapy

Pink and peachy kisses blotted on tissues, promising a woman's world. She always looked so pretty.

Lipstick.

It's cheaper than therapy.

It's a Phase

The title of this chapter may seem self-evident for any parent with a youngster who has reached age three. But stay tuned: the second child brings new twists to this little truism.

In the first few years with Isabelle, all my parenting problems seemed permanent. When she wouldn't poop on the potty at two, I envisioned a kindergartner in diapers. When she refused to give up her bottle, I thought orthodontics. I couldn't imagine how I'd survive motherhood without sleeping again.

By Jessica's birth, I'd seen enough problems pass to realize that most of motherhood's challenges are temporary. Like other veteran moms, my mantra became "It's a phase." Jessica wants only milk? Let it be. The little one sucks her thumb? This, too, shall pass. Early on, two kids proved an endurance test. However, my perspective on parenting was more developed, the Buddhist tenet of impermanence having finally hit home. It's a phase, and you can even outlast some phases, watching to-dos like "Buy walker" fall off the list from sheer neglect. The house and kids were dirtier than they had been with one child, but little by little I was becoming enlightened.

Then Jessica turned two.

On a steamy Saturday night in June, Bill and I dine out, and then stop by Borders. I head for the parenting section.

A mom beyond one has to be desperate to spend date night with Spock and Sears. But for a month now, ever since she turned two, Jessica has been throwing wardrobe tantrums. Just as her sister did, she's melting down over pink and purple, getting violent over pockets, and ripping off her clothes just as we're about to leave home.

As an experienced mother of daughters, I know this is a phase. However, I don't want to be in this phase. Isabelle's terrible twos only recently ended and I hated them. My older girl had just begun dressing herself without tears and tantrums when Jessica started tearing off her outfits. And this time, it's more difficult because I've got two children to get out the door, and the wardrobe bug is contagious. No sooner has Jessica flung a shoe at my head than my four year old starts to wonder about her shoes too. Socks get itchy. Shorts feel tight. Then the whole princess panties thing starts.

It's the good news and bad news of having another child: you get to do it all again. Some things are sweeter and more fleeting the second time around. Others, however, grow more tedious with a repeat performance. And that adage about becoming more patient with time? Forget it. Patience is definitely an exhaustible resource. Isabelle's twos used most of mine up.

So on our Saturday night out, I turn to my buddy Vicki Iovine. *The Girlfriends' Guide to Getting Your Groove Back*, after all, proved life changing for one whole night. I'm hoping for a little more groove as I open Iovine's toddler tome. Instead I find this: "By the time you have a toddler, you realize that not only is your life not about you right now, it's not going to be about you for the foreseeable future."

No, Vicki, no!

I sink into the couch. Borders' spiritual section is around the corner, but it seems unreachable. I know, having watched Isabelle transform from a terrible two into a terrific three, that this isn't permanent. I understand, this time, that my two year old won't end up with a closet like Imelda Marcos.

But I also know that the wardrobe battles last a year, and that the next one is scheduled for eight A.M.

It takes five tries the next morning to get Jessica's dress on for church, four wardrobe showdowns in the afternoon when she insists on another outfit for a party. Inspired by her younger sister, Isabelle repeatedly changes clothes too. I'm tired, feel cranky, and have my panties on backward as we arrive at the barbeque.

Munching pretzels with one hand, sipping wine with the other, a mom with older children smiles down at my pink-clad girls and coos, "Oh, it goes too fast!"

I balance a plate of kiddie finger food with ten napkins and two juices and think, *Give me a break.*

Dinnertime, 1970s style. My mother is making meatloaf. My stepfather, twelve-year-old brother, and I sit at the kitchen table. The TV presents medics carrying soldiers on stretchers and wailing villagers. American boys are coming home in body bags. Looking grim, Walter Cronkite gives the day's death count. At fifteen, I sit riveted.

My mother leaves the room and returns with a redheaded toddler. Plopping him into a high chair by our table, she dishes out Gerber's applesauce. *BANG! BANG! BANG!* goes the baby spoon on the bowl. "*Whaaa!!!*"

Walter doesn't have a chance. With a flip of the channel, a dark-haired man speaking in soothing tones of a neighborhood quickly replaces him. For the rest of dinner, we watch Mr. Rogers.

The mothers at the park considering another pregnancy always ask about spacing, as if there were a magical age difference for familial harmony. Experts advocate a wide range of gaps; every scenario has its pluses and minuses.

Generally, spacing kids less than three years apart means they can play together and will like to do the same things. But it can be hell on parents early on. Expert Burton White's admonition, which I read while pregnant with Jessica, still rings in my ear: "The single greatest source of stress on families with more than one child is close (less than three years) spacing of children. No matter how able and energetic you are, close spacing in almost every case will make your job remarkably more difficult and less rewarding."

Wider spacing is easier on parents at first and allows each child to get more attention. However, siblings will not have the same interests early on. That doesn't mean they won't get along, though: sibling compatibility depends more on personality than on spacing. And contrary to popular belief, neither birth order nor age difference between siblings has a critical effect on personality and adjustment.

What is guaranteed, however, is that although every kid is a blessing, each is also a huge step backward for their parents. *When* you take that step backward determines how long phases feel, how rapidly they seem to pass, and how many years you're an on-the-job mom or dad. It's a phase. Yet some phases can feel permanent the second or third time around.

I missed a lot of the Vietnam War as a result of having a half-brother fourteen years younger than me. My mother missed more. Her kids' wide spacing meant that when my stepfather and I partied late on vacation, she stayed in the room to nurse my younger brother's fever. It meant that when we went skiing, she stayed in the lodge.

My mom did well with this—she hated skiing anyway, didn't harbor career ambitions, and easily kept up with the younger moms. She also raised a delightful young man, whom it's difficult, now, to imagine life without. But our fourteen-year gap meant that, for better and worse, my mother had children at home for more than thirty years. When her oldest child left for college, her youngest was just starting kindergarten.

The step I take in reverse is tiny in comparison, making me marvel at my mom's vaulting leap back to the diaper-changing table. On days when the shoes fly and Jessica pees on the floor, though, I feel it nonetheless. The moms who stopped with one have all graduated, moving on to diaper-free outings and tantrum-free dinners. As Jessica disrobes, a postcard arrives from the Greek island of Samos, where my friend Sara is traveling with her only child, who was in Isabelle's baby group. I haven't felt so arrested since I moved to a cinder-block dorm room for graduate school in Missouri while my friends rented apartments in Washington D.C. and New York City.

So I have conflicting feelings toward my second as she turns two. Her sweet moments run like sand through my fingers. Yet she's also holding the entire family back. Traveling together, for instance, often isn't worth the expense—with Jessica now big enough to require a paid airline seat, but still small enough to ruin the trip.

My second child is a gift from the gods, but there's no doubt about it: if we'd stopped with Isabelle, we'd be doing a lot more by now.

June turns to July. I learn little at Borders about toddlers that I didn't know before. Jessica wants to wear her yellow dress—every day. Hand-me-downs start backfiring. Why it took me one whole child to learn to buy Velcro I don't know, but Jessica insists on wearing Isabelle's old black patent leather shoes, which she desperately wants but cannot buckle herself. Then the summer rains begin.

It always rains in Miami in July. This year, however, it rains all day, every day. Everywhere you go, people talk about the rain. Parents are particularly desperate. Even the chipper moms at the dentist's office look gloomy. The saving grace with kids in summer in south Florida is that you can usually wait out the rain and swim. This July, it's hard to even leave home, and the little ones have cabin fever.

Jessica and Isabelle tear up the house. Tempers flare. I feel more claustrophobic than I did in any northern winter. Even snow pants, with those last-minute gotta-pee problems, look good. When the University of Indiana at Bloomington calls Bill to discuss a law-school position, we schedule a visit for the fall.

Bloomington has the charms of a university town, and as we arrive without the kids a few months later, the leaves are changing color. I take long baths in the hotel room, read Edna St. Vincent Millay's biography, and dine with faculty. Exploring, I find a stable, where a friendly mom and her eight-year-old daughter are riding. A host of equestrian fantasies surface as I imagine my girls trotting on horses over southern Indiana's rolling hills.

We return from the trip excited. Bill prints out everything on the Internet on Bloomington. Our Midwest relatives call, asking our plans. Academic appointments take years, and for my husband to be seriously considered for the position he would have to visit for a semester—a major inconvenience. Yet I sense that it could be a go.

Then November arrives. It's a long time coming this year, but Miami finally takes its schizophrenic leap from humid hot-house to tropical paradise. The East Coast endures a bitter winter. In an act of God, our daughters are both accepted at our church's school, a small, excellent institution close to home.

Approaching three, Jessica emerges from her room one day fully dressed, her shoes on the correct feet, her dress purple and without pockets—the lack of which led to many an earlier meltdown. "I did it all by myself," she grins.

The next summer, rain pours down. But we do not discuss Bloomington—at all.

Late August, six-thirty A.M. Today there will be no wardrobe battles, no pleading over pockets, no meltdowns over shoes.

I have been guarding them in my office like vestments. Now I bring them downstairs and carefully lay them out: the school uniforms.

Jessica, who will be in the nursery, is going to school for the first time. Isabelle is starting kindergarten. It's a new phase, and I'm nervous about the schedule. But I love the dress code.

Wardrobe choices eliminated, the girls put on their clothes quickly. Jessica isn't sure about school. However, after hearing about her classroom's baby dolls, she perks up. In a record forty minutes, they're out the door.

The house is strangely quiet as the girls leave with Bill. I wander for a moment, disoriented. I didn't even used to be up at this hour, but then, getting them to bed at eight-thirty is revolutionary too.

I knew it was a phase—the period of time before Jessica went to school when Bill and I read to our little one every morning before Nancy came. I remember lots of shoe fits, how I craved on occasion to eat breakfast alone, how—as one toddler phase lapped into another—I tired of panty and pocket rebellions. I have yet to get my groove back and still can't find some of my makeup.

On this first morning of nursery school, though, I'm thinking not of the wailing, but of the giggling that filled the house at this hour a breath ago. By eight it's so quiet that when I turn on the *Today Show*, it echoes off the walls.

I missed the beginning of the Iraq war reading Barney. I don't recognize the flavor of the month in the TV interview.

However, there's talk of Iran's harboring weapons of mass destruction. Another Mideast peace plan has gone up in flames. The morning shows have more ads than I remember.

I take a shower. No one asks to join me. I go up to my office early. No one beckons me down.

Some phases are sweeter the second time around. Some wear worse with repetition. Others seem to stretch endlessly, despite the savviest spacing.

They all pass.

The parents arrive early at the nursery-school pickup, chatting outside the school about their little charges, wondering how it went.

I'm the first one there.

Dreaming of Divorce

I am fantasizing about divorcing my husband.

This also happened with the advent of my first child. But then my reasons were more traditional. I just didn't see, at times, how I could continue to live with a man who could not multitask in the kitchen.

Now, with two kids, I want to get divorced so I can date the guy I see but do not speak to. Two and four are not as civilized as they sound from one and three. Jessica is having loud toddler meltdowns. Isabelle has taken over the stereo. My sister-in-law, who has one child, talks to her husband over dinner while her son plays with his trucks. But with two, Bill might as well live on Mars. Though he stands nearby, I can't hear a word he says. And if there is one thing I don't like, it's living with a man with whom I can't talk.

Look, I tell him one night. It makes perfect sense. We get divorced and alternate weekends with the kids, dating in between. We do the logistics by email and talk and make out when we get together.

"I don't think this is the answer," he replies.

Bill doesn't get it. His parents stayed married. Mine divorced. And during her three years as a single lady, my mother lived well. Handsome men took her to dinner. My father took my brother and me Saturday and Sunday, giving her weekends free. Then she remarried, providing us with a stepfather and the proper parental ratio for two kids: three to two.

Of course it's hard for many single moms who are divorced. My mother had good financial support. But mothers who remarry sometimes do well. I go green just listening to their talk of weekend getaways with their mates. They've got the answer for every baby-sitting dilemma: Dad. Bill and I have had two nights away alone in four years. Baby-sitting for a whole weekend is prohibitively expensive, and since we have childcare weekdays, we hate to use it much on weekends. Leaving the kids with Dad, though, is different. And imagine alternating holidays. Every other Christmas off!

I want a divorce.

Bill points out that even with a divorce we still wouldn't have anybody to take the kids while we traveled. And what about the children?

And what about them? When my mother remarried, I inherited three new uncles, one aunt, three cousins, and four more grandparents, my stepfather having stepparents himself. My parents' divorce provided me with more relatives than any kid I knew.

My husband looks tired. We're finally having a weeknight conversation and I'm ranting about divorce? He points out that the kids won't have new relatives unless one of us remarries.

Well, okay. And I guess there are some other problems. If we divorce, I won't get to see Isabelle try to squeeze Bill into a tutu or watch him court Jessica for a kiss.

Still, I can't help but fantasize. The next morning, as I bark over Barney for Bill to remember the lunch box, I see her again: the woman who read *The Wizard of Oz* to my brother and me on weeknights and dated on weekends.

Friends with older children tell me to cool my jets. Their marriages became rocky when their kids were this age. My informal survey shows that ages two and four are when parents do couples therapy. Yet those same friends seem happy now. And I can't bear the thought of missing the dress-up-Daddy scenes.

So I bag the divorce idea and settle for the next-best thing: an affair.

Okay, it's not extramarital. But it's clandestine. Cunning and an exquisite sense of timing are required to get Nancy out with Jessica, some writing done, and my man naked up in my office before the preschool pickup—on a day when my law professor husband doesn't teach or have a faculty meeting and the handyman isn't around.

I don't get my dream divorce. However, the soft whir of the computer hard drive provides a delicious feeling of doing something illicit.

I guess if I'm after the fellow I'm married to, it will all work out.

Breathe In, Breathe Out

Many parents with a firstborn preschooler or toddler and a second baby discover a new side of themselves, one they don't always like.

—JUDY DUNN, *From One Child to Two*

"ISABELLE, COME RIGHT NOW OR YOU ARE GOING INTO TIME-OUT! ONE, TWO . . ." The bark blasting down the hallway is as loud as a drill sergeant's, but angrier. And it's mine.

While pregnant with Jessica, I read about a study that showed a striking rise in confrontation between mothers and firstborns after the birth of a second child. Parents are typically tougher on their first after a new arrival—some experts believe too tough. Not me, I thought. No way am I going to scream at my precious Isabelle.

Now as my four year old refuses to brush her teeth at bedtime, yelling is tame compared to what I really want to do: throw her out the window. Jessica drives me nuts too, and the increased chaos in the house since her birth has also fed my newborn temper. But Isabelle takes the heat. Because she is older, I expect more of her. Behavior that was once amusing is annoying when you have two kids to manage. Landing in my lap with a forty-pound thud as I read to Jessica, my big girl makes me furious.

Growing up, I thought my own mother yelled too often. Now I don't know why she didn't yell more. How else to get kids' attention when you've asked them to eat their cereal in a nice voice five times? And what tactic more effective when you don't believe in spanking? A few good mommy shouts and bingo—those teeth are pearly white, and shoes get put away too. A major mommy scream will even untangle flailing limbs in time to eat dinner hot. And the mommy meltdowns? I'm not proud of them, but afterward my little ones act like angels.

Since having a second, I've also noticed that lots of other moms scream too. "Yell?" responds a girlfriend with two older children, sounding as blasé as if I'd mentioned a trip to the grocery store. "I do it all the time." In *Parenting* magazine, writer Paula Spencer notes that while yelling usually doesn't work, it's hard to avoid and occasionally has benefits, getting kids' attention when all else fails and releasing pent-up parental anger. Writes Spencer, who has four: "Sometimes, letting loose just makes a mom feel good—and shouldn't that count for something?" And in another *Parenting* article, mother of three and pediatrician Perri Klass makes a confession before offering some better approaches for discipline: "I yell at my kids. I yell in the house, sometimes closing the windows so the neighbors can't hear. I yell in the car. I try not to yell in public, but I'm great at that poisonous, through-the-teeth hiss that's almost as good."

My husband doesn't yell. But then, he goes to the bathroom alone and enjoys exclusive use of his toiletries. The kids are also never wilder than when he puts them to bed. Lately I find myself wishing—can it be?—for a deep male bellow down the hall at night indicating that Bill is in control rather than that calm daddy voice and the scuffle of little feet, with Isabelle shouting, "Quick, Jessica, run!"

Yet if yelling has advantages and seems natural with a clan, its drawbacks reverberate too. The voice of conscience is four years old. "You're not speaking in a nice voice," says Isabelle after gentle cajoling fails and I shout during bedtime again. Gotcha.

And though it feels good to let off steam, afterward I suffer a double whammy: mad at them, mad at myself. How did this happen? Before having two, I considered myself easygoing. I haven't been so out of control since dealing with Nicaraguan bureaucrats over car registration. Then, as now, blasting people, big or small, while momentarily satisfying, leaves me ashamed.

Oh well, I figure, tucking Isabelle in after her call to conscience. We'll both get over the evening's shouting. Children are amazingly resilient. Once my older daughter's head hits the pillow, she's out like a light. Isabelle always seems to recover from my anger faster than I do.

Then the next morning, I hear it—the neighbors probably do too—a four-year-old drill sergeant with a ferocious bark: "JESSICA, IF YOU DON'T COME HERE RIGHT NOW, YOU'RE GETTING A TIME-OUT!"

"*Whaaaa!*" screams my youngest, running to me terrified.

If only Jessica knew.

It's a few days later, and my vow is firm: I will not lose my temper. I will not raise my voice.

Parenting expert Sal Severe is my guide. After Isabelle began yelling at Jessica, I read his book, *How to Behave So Your Preschooler Will, Too,* the title and Severe's credentials as a school psychologist and father of four having caught my eye.

Severe confirmed what I had suspected: since children imitate their parents, yelling begets yelling. He says adult screaming also shows kids that they can manipulate their folks. "Getting angry is one of the most common problems parents face, and it is the largest stumbling block in our relationship with our children," writes the psychologist. Managing anger is key to effective parenting: to keep cool, Severe says, parents should identify in advance behaviors that trigger anger and take responsibility for their reactions.

As I warm milk for Jessica before reading bedtime stories, the note on the refrigerator that reads "Stay Calm" reinforces my resolve. My commitment stands. I will give Isabelle as many time-outs as needed. I will take away her penny collection, if necessary. But I will not yell, even as the big trigger approaches: the great nightie meltdown.

Breathe in. Breathe out. "Isabelle," I start calmly. "I've already asked you to come three times. I am going to start reading now." It's a behavior that sets off many parents: repeating things like a parrot and being ignored until you try to do something else.

"NO!"

Isabelle wants help putting on her nightgown. I've already tried four times. She is old enough to dress herself. It's not about the nightgown.

Breathe in. Breathe out. Bill is at a meeting. Just as well.

I continue reading to Jessica, "A mother bird sat on her egg. . . ."

"NO! NO! NO!" screams Isabelle. "I don't want that book! I want *my* book first!"

I keep reading. Isabelle erupts, yelling at the top of her lungs. Grabbing my bathrobe, she tries to pull me off the couch. I remove her hands and continue, "The egg jumped."

Screaming, Isabelle runs to her room and slams the door. *BANG. CRASH.* I hear objects flying. *SLAM!* The bureau drawer. Did she break it? Damn, just what I need to do: fix furniture.

Read. Just keep reading, "'Oh, oh!' said the mother bird. 'My baby will be here! He will want to eat.'"

I can barely hear my own words over Isabelle's raging, though Jessica, sitting in the catbird's seat, is remarkably calm. Severe's advice comes back to me: "Use a delay strategy to weaken the effects of the trigger event. Count to twenty-five or practice deep breathing. Meditate. Think peaceful thoughts. Say a prayer for tolerance and forgiveness. . . ."

Continuing to read the bedtime story, I make a decision: as long as it's Isabelle, not me, getting angry, it's okay. I don't care when they get to bed. I don't care how loud or how long she screams. I have only one goal: to stay calm.

mmmm . . .

Then suddenly, as my oldest rants, I feel something strange. I'm free. Her yelling is no longer my problem. Isabelle has lost control over me.

Ten minutes? Twenty minutes? Five hours? An apparition in a nightgown appears on the edge of the couch. Inch by tearful inch, she moves closer.

"Are you ready for your book?" I ask.

Sniffle. Sniffle. "Yes," she answers, curling up beside me like a kitten.

We read and cuddle. I brush their teeth and put them to bed.

The next night bedtime goes like clockwork.

God, this is better than meditation.

The square-faced, balding man at the bookstore looks strangely familiar. And though we've never met, he seems like a confidant. Who is this fellow? Then I remember the author's photo.

Sal Severe is visiting Miami and has stopped in the store to sign books. There are none to sign; he's sold out. Nervously, I approach him.

"Listen, I want to thank you. I read *How to Behave So Your Preschooler Will, Too.* The advice about yelling was really helpful. The other night my four year old had a tantrum. But I didn't!"

"That's wonderful! Good for you!" he says, smiling.

Now, if I'd known, years ago, that I'd be bragging about not throwing a tantrum to a nationally renowned parenting expert, I might not have had kids in the first place.

Yet there's nothing like lowering the bar to bring parental accomplishment and satisfaction within reach.

Wonderful? Good? They were the psychologist's words, not mine.

Call them second-rate, slipshod standards. Yet, when a mom with a clan can keep her cool, she definitely deserves an accolade or two.

Memory

We've got him flanked.

My brother Jon sits on one side of the hospital bed holding my father's hand. I sit on the other, hand on Dad's arm. For days we've been manning these positions, trying to coax our sedated father toward health. Now the game is over. In a morning meeting with the doctors, my brother and I, along with my dad's girlfriend, Fran, have made the ultimate decision. Slowly, the doctors are lowering the oxygen levels on Dad's ventilator to "room air."

Who could have imagined? When I visited my father after his hip surgery a few weeks earlier, he was fine. Soon after, however, he contracted double pneumonia, and his condition deteriorated from there. A virus too? Complications from his Parkinson's? We'll never know for sure. Only one thing is certain: my father will not end up at a nursing home connected to a ventilator and a feeding tube. On this, with the support of Fran, Jon and I have agreed.

So we sit with him for a few moments before going down to the lobby to make the difficult calls. I talk to the aunts. Jon phones our uncle. Then, bracing ourselves against the cold, we walk to lunch. My brother reminds me of the physician's prognosis regarding Dad's condition: a slim chance for survival, slimmer yet of living as he had before. I recall my father's words during an earlier medical crisis: "I'd rather be dead than not drive." We've done the right thing; he had a living will. Yet who can forget that miraculous moment a few days earlier when Dad opened his eyes and flashed *each* of us a brilliant smile? It's hard, very hard. And just so cold.

It's early April, yet snow is falling, a blizzard expected by nightfall. Later, my brother stays with my father while I stroll down a street I played on as a child. It's beautiful, silent, and haunting: my father liked warmth, not cold. "I'm sick of the white stuff," he'd said just a month earlier after yet another snowstorm. Many things will never seem the same again. One of them is snow.

For days, my brother and I have been walking these streets. It's strange being back in Connecticut, where we spent part of our childhoods. We haven't visited these neighborhoods together since we were kids. "Remember smoking Salems in this graveyard?" I asked a few days earlier, when Dad's vital signs were positive enough to enjoy a ramble down memory lane. "This is where he picked us up in that little blue VW Bug," my brother noted, standing in front of the house we lived in with my mother after our parents divorced. Jon felt the same way: everything looked so small. Only the stones in the graveyard behind that house seemed unchanged.

Now, walking alone, I dare not linger. The doctors have said it can take anywhere from one hour to two weeks for someone in Dad's state to die once life support is removed. Bracing myself, I return to my father's room. As he has every day, Jon gives me the latest stats. Oxygen and blood pressure levels are dropping, beeps from the machines marking their descent. No one runs to check them anymore.

I take my place on one side of the bed. The nurses have removed many of the intravenous lines, making it easier for my brother to hold one of Dad's hands and for me to hold the other.

On a TV overhead, the battle for Baghdad unfolds. By the bed the ventilator's rhythm slows. Outside it snows and snows.

In the morning, there are eight inches on the ground and our father is dead.

Death makes it clear. I should have spent more time with him.

My father and I were close, but I didn't see him much after Jessica's birth. With a new baby, and then, as she grew, two toddlers, it was more difficult to get away, harder to call. Taking one small child to Connecticut had been doable; taking two felt insurmountable. The year before his death, I brought my dad to Florida to see the kids, but the visit was long overdue. "You're where you need to be," my father had said every time I'd apologized for my absence. And yet, had I been?

My brother consoles me, as does the memory of a wonderful day spent with my father four months earlier. The picture I took then is at home, but Jon has it on his laptop: a sterling shot of Dad sporting his slightly crooked half-smile on a crystal clear day at his favorite spot by the sea. My brother emails it to the newspaper, together with the obituary. April 8, 2003. Seventy-six years old. "There's a date out there for all of us," says Jon.

My brother sits on the sofa bed Dad used to sleep on when, as kids, we visited him in his New York apartment. I'm in our father's command center, his worn easy chair. On the desk lies a last to-do list: "Call Jon. Call Jen. Buy hearing-aid batteries." In the bedroom, Dad's glasses rest on the bureau, change lies on the table.

Jon phones the funeral home. I riffle though old letters looking for friends to call. And as we sit, surrounded by his things, I think, Wouldn't it be horrible to do this alone?

In the weeks that follow, Jon orders the Dumpster. I phone the old friends. My brother gets the blue-book value on the car. I sort out the hospital bills.

But later I realize it isn't just having the help, critical as our teamwork is. And it isn't even that, as we fly in to fill the Dumpster in three frantic rainy days in order to turn over Dad's house to his landlord, we manage to laugh. Comic relief, however, does prove as essential as commiseration. ("What about the guns!? You can't ship guns!" my brother exclaims, walking out of Dad's bedroom with two vintage rifles. "Guns?!" I howl, before running off with him to the local dealer for a full-blown discourse on weaponry, sister and brother surrounded by duck hunting gear and stifling giggles like two kids in a crowded elevator.)

As two, we can take turns being strong, pull each other through. Buried somewhere in my filing cabinet, it surfaces in my brother's, the detailed medical directive with specific instructions in my father's wiry handwriting, further validating our decision. Yet somehow, I would manage alone. People without siblings do.

However, an only child couldn't have the conversation that Jon and I do cleaning out Dad's closet. For if many know a man, only a sibling knows the father.

"Hey Jen," says my brother, holding up a jacket as we go through Dad's clothes. "Isn't this the one he used to wear on those visits? Can't you just see Dad in this, waving out the car window?"

I gaze at the worn beige jacket, run my fingers down its soft corduroy strands, then look at Jon. And for a moment we're standing on our grandparents' front steps again, two kids holding back tears, watching a dark-haired man in a beige corduroy jacket wave goodbye.

Back home, after I've spent almost two weeks in the intensive-care unit, their skin seems so velvety, their youth so brilliant.

Yet as one plays Ariel and the other mimics Snow White, it's their adult conversation that I imagine. It's easy to forget in these early years raising kids: the enduring tie is the sibling bond, not the parental one. Someday, if my prayer is answered, my children's main link to me will be each other.

In the following weeks, emails fly back and forth between the coasts. "I miss the voice," says my brother. "I can't believe I'll never hear that voice again." Dad's voice: deep, wise, gentle, listening, so supportive of his kids. I miss it too.

Memory can't bring him back. But it does help make up for losses, big and small.

Who cares if Jessica and Isabelle fight over the marbles, if someday one sister can lead the other back to me?

Incompletion

"Self-help for moms" is an oxymoron. The more kids you have, the more implausible the idea seems. For a busy mom with a growing family, even the female self-help writers' advice is as achievable as a trip to Tahiti. In *Feel the Fear and Do It Anyway*, Susan Jeffers suggests listening to inspirational tapes upon rising: "Lie with your eyes closed and let the soothing, loving messages sink in." Yeah, right.

Still, if each additional child makes self-help and the order, control, and achievement it promises more elusive, each also makes it more enticing. As the family grows, I crave order more. The experts advise parents to accept that they can't control as much of life as they'd like when the kids are young. But the psychologists say it's control that makes us happy. With Jessica and Isabelle now three and five, I'm ready for a little more. I've lived with chaos and low expectations for years. It's time to raise the bar. After all, the kids are developing. Can't I?

My latest guide is *The Power of Full Engagement* by Jim Loehr and Tony Schwartz. By studying elite athletes and other high achievers, the authors have found that it's best to manage your time according to your energy level and establish specific rituals to achieve your goals. Precise plans, they note, make a difference. In one study they describe, women were asked to do a breast self-examination the following month. Almost all who made specific plans to do the exam did it, compared to only 53 percent of those without such plans.

No wonder some of my goals aren't getting accomplished. I keep vowing to lose another ten pounds and write more but haven't figured out how to achieve these aims.

So I create a plan. I know better than to be ambitious. Two years earlier, inspired by a stretch in which everyone slept through the night, I spent two hours of precious free time elaborately planning my week with Stephen Covey's book *First Things First.* Covey distinguishes between importance and urgency, and advises scheduling blocks of time for critical matters and fitting the rest of life around those. Days later, I ripped up my schedule after the kids took it over, a host of small concerns such as finding Jessica's blankie and running out for milk proving both urgent and important.

But Loehr and Schwartz advise starting slowly, incorporating new rituals over time. So I set three modest goals. First, I plan to increase my writing time by starting work earlier in the mornings and afternoons, ignoring my email and the phone while writing, and doing more paperwork in the evenings. Second, I vow to do more free weights at the gym by leaving my office fifteen minutes earlier each day. And finally, I plan to count Weight Watchers points by recording them after each meal instead of at day's end, when memory lapses and motivation lags.

Here's how it goes:

Monday. Success! Counting Weight Watcher points, I discover I'm eating a lot more than before. Good news? Bad? I'm not sure, but it's a revelation. As usual, I'm slow getting up to my office, playing with Jessica until she goes to the park with Nancy at ten. Yet by ignoring the phone and email, I write longer. Later, at the gym, I bump my exercise routine up from pathetic to real.

Feeling buff upon returning home, I hear an earth-shattering scream. "*WHAAAAA!*"

In the bedroom, my husband looks pale. "Isabelle flipped backwards off the bed and hit her head on the floor," he says gravely, as my oldest staggers into my arms. Quickly, we shift into crisis mode. Bill dashes to the bookshelf to read about head injuries, then calls the pediatrician. I scramble to comfort Isabelle while cooking dinner, determined not to take a hungry child to the emergency room.

Meanwhile, Jessica collapses on the floor in a toddler rage, frustrated because she can't get the Ariel costume on. Covey had one thing right: what appears urgent isn't always important. While Isabelle lies peacefully on the couch, Jessica sounds like she's dying.

The doctor says that Isabelle is probably okay but advises waking her up every few hours to be sure she's coherent.

The paperwork doesn't get done that evening. Yet I'm thrilled when, asked her name at one A.M., my oldest mumbles: "Isabelle."

Tuesday. It's morning writing time. It's also the last day of preschool. I'd meant to write the teachers' thank-you notes last night but nursed my oldest instead. The notes aren't a do-or-die matter. Little of the stuff in my life is. Like most moms, though, I have a lot of it.

I finish the cards and am preparing to write when my brother Jon calls. I've vowed not to talk during writing time. But what can I say? My relationships with my brothers are one reason I wanted another child. I hope that Jessica interrupts Isabelle's work someday too.

I do eventually start writing, quite late. I also count Weight Watchers points. Quite high. I was just there with my little ones, but the dentist claims Mommy's teeth need to be cleaned too. After a quick lunch, I drive over.

Actually, I shouldn't protest. Daisy, my hygienist, has two older children, making her a great two-for-one. I get my teeth cleaned and receive good parenting advice in the process. From Oops-a-Daisy, as my kids call her, I've learned to buy stickers by the dozen and where to shop for secondhand kids' clothes. Hearing this together mom admit to initially wanting to throw her first baby out the window helped me handle Jessica's colic. I've learned more from Oops-a-Daisy than from Spock, Leach, and Sears combined.

Today the hygienist looks exceptionally chipper as she recommends Sarah Ban Breathnach's book *Romancing the Ordinary*. Hmmm. Breathnach's bestselling *Simple Abundance* inspired me to make three trips to the Container Store. Yet the morning that Jessica and Isabelle covered the kitchen floor with oatmeal, I concluded that many of her ideas are currently beyond reach. Breathnach is the mother of one daughter—a nice, civilized eight year old when she began the book. My abundance is not as simple as that of Sarah Ban Breathnach.

But Oops-a-Daisy has two kids and is also reading *The Complete Idiot's Guide to Understanding Buddhism:* perhaps there's hope. Promising to give the book a try, I leave, cavity-free.

In my absence, Nancy picks Isabelle up from school. As I return home, my older girl hugs me, then bounds off to play. After reading to Jessica, I'm preparing to go up to my office and work when the mommy alarm sounds.

The inner clock I've developed since having my second is a marvel of mommy instinct and ingenuity. Incredibly precise, it tracks time spent with each daughter and sounds when one gets behind. Isabelle's head injury put her in the lead. My little one's expression, and the fact that I don't have a major deadline, revamps my plan. So I read *Amelia Bedelia* and *Toot & Puddle,* then refine our peekaboo game to include some roughhousing. Jessica squeals in delight. When I finally get up to my office, I feel behind but blessed—exactly how I feel most of the time.

Later, I think of writing "Jessica, thirty pounds" on my gym chart as I complete a fifteen-minute workout. "Leaving already?" asks the gym receptionist, confused since she just checked me in.

Yes. And today, I need no excuse for skipping the free weights.

Wednesday. This morning, Isabelle has a cough. Most people sleep more when they're sick. Isabelle sleeps less. At six A.M. she's in my bed. It's wonderfully cozy at first: I love cuddling my firstborn alone. Then the questions begin: "Is Peter Pan real? Why not? How does he fly? What about Tinkerbell? Can

I have a Tinkerbell birthday party? How much longer until my birthday? Let's decorate the house today!"

Now I remember why I put off motherhood: I'm not a morning person. Although my female friends wanted their lovers to speak to them in the morning, I always said the same thing: don't bother. In the early hours, I'm a woman of few words. Kids, though, won't take no for an answer, and so, since having two, I've become an aficionado of the morning shows, watching for some clue on how these amazing TV personalities keep their mouths moving. No insights have emerged, but I have decided one thing: Katie Couric deserves her millions. This is hard work and I don't even have to do my hair. Having risen repeatedly the other night to check Isabelle's breathing, I'm shot.

Later, foggy in my office, I can't quite remember what I'm supposed to do. I also don't recall what I ate, but then, the extra ten: why lose them? Counting Weight Watchers points looks like a resolution made from another, rarefied, reality. I don't even like the kind of woman who writes down what she eats. All I want to count are sheep.

So I open my book project to-do list. One thing I've learned in recent years is to note steps on an undertaking for guidance on foggy mommy days. Loehr and Schwartz suggest planning your time around your energy levels. With small children, though, energy highs and lows are hard to predict. This is prime time for my writing, yet the only storyline in my head is *Peter Pan*. Looking for something doable on the list, I find "Call Gwen for book thoughts."

Yes! My cousin Gwen lives outside of Chicago and has two girls, one six and the other a baby. She's also trained as a teacher. Best of all, I can always count on her for a laugh.

When I call, Gwen's husband says she is painting the hallway.

Painting the hallway? Gwen is home with her kids and though her husband often works out of the house and pitches in, she doesn't have any other help. They also have two large dogs.

I'm thinking spilled paint, paw prints, sticky fingers, and poison control when she answers the phone.

"Are you really painting the hall?" I ask.

"I am," she answers, explaining that she's doing the hallway in ten-minute increments. "I've also been doing the yard work for short periods, but that's worse because you spend more time cleaning up than raking leaves." Since having her second, Gwen says she's done most of her projects in short bursts, having lost the predictable blocks of free time she'd had with only one child.

"I love to start projects and finish them," says my cousin. "But forget it. With two, it's impossible to plan your day. You can't say, I'm going to do yard work from nine to ten. You learn to live with incompletion."

Time snatched. Piecemeal projects. Messes. Gear switching. Revising plans on a dime. A sense of incompletion, even as life is more complete than ever before. This doesn't sound like *The Power of Full Engagement*, but it sounds a lot like my life.

I couldn't write a book or even an article in ten-minute segments—which is why we have childcare. Bill and I have also structured our lives to give each other blocks of time. Even so, with two small kids, my plans are constantly being blown out of the water. Like Gwen's, my life is a series of interruptions, half-finished projects, and incremental steps to push an increasing number of balls forward.

Gwen seems to have made peace with her chaos. Why can't I?

Thursday. Before Jessica claimed my other hand and remaining free minutes, I used to cook in the traditional manner. That is, I would start something, finish it, and eat it while it was hot.

Now I cook in steps. This morning, as I watch Jessica and make my coffee, I am doing step one for my adulterated version of Weight Watchers Spinach and Cheese Quiche. I put nonfat cottage cheese, parmesan, nonfat condensed milk, and four eggs in a bowl and store it in the fridge. Later, when I make my afternoon coffee, I'll defrost a box of spinach, and add salt and pepper to the egg concoction. Some morning when the kids wake me up early, I'll bake a piecrust, let Isabelle drain the spinach and line the crust with it, pour in the egg concoction, and bake it.

Making spinach quiche this way takes several days. But it also allows me to make the entire quiche without spending one extra minute in my least favorite place in the house: the kitchen. The same piecemeal approach allows me to do a manicure without spending much time in the bathroom and get the presents wrapped without staying up until two A.M. on Christmas Eve. As with Gwen, there's method in my madness.

The result, however, is a lot of loose ends. Leaving the unfinished quiche, I go upstairs to face the partly written book, the half-revised magazine essay, and my dad's confused car papers, which I've tried repeatedly, without success, to sort out.

However, today I've had eight hours of sleep. Having gotten up with Isabelle at six, Bill is staggering around the house, coughing. But I'm cruising. My Weight Watchers points are still high, but falling. I turn off my email, ignore the phone, and write for two hours. After picking up Isabelle from school and reading stories to the kids midday, I finally solve the car papers problem. Then I revise the essay, sending it in ahead of schedule.

For the first time in weeks, I finish things. Not the pie, but the essay, the car papers, the Weight Watchers points—I'm kicking ass. Today I feel like I've got life mastered.

And this is the problem.

Friday. Walking to the gym, I recall Gwen saying, "You have to do a little bit at a time and learn that it's okay."

Approaching the free weights, though, I do not feel okay. I see it on my exercise chart: the bicep curl. I hate the bicep curl. It's boring and hard. I don't want to be here, and, in fact, I'm not. My head is in the book that I left in the midst of a burst of inspiration because it was time to go to the gym because later we're taking the kids to dinner because we need family time, and I desperately want to get out of the house and away from my computer and all this planning and structure and counting and calculating and crap.

I didn't predict a burst of writing energy at four P.M. Writing well in the afternoon is not part of the plan, which at this point is so well laid out, with so many people, that it's not worth changing. I once read of a novelist who didn't want children because she wanted to be able to write through the night when the spirit moved her. Today, I understand.

So I haul out a seventeen-pound weight for the bicep curl. It's heavier than the one I usually use. I'm not thinking about that, though. I'm worried about losing my brilliant thoughts. The little notebook in my gym fanny pack is gone—probably in the same place as the missing red earring and pink lipstick.

Damn, but I want completion! I want to finish just one thing and cross it off my to-do list. I want to be in the moment I'm in—which right now means writing the book, not pumping iron. Barring this, I want, at least, to record my ideas so I can find them again.

I thought, when Jessica was a baby and I scribbled notes for projects on wet scrap paper while giving her a bath, that the problem of shifting gears would be a short phase. I imagined that when my younger girl gave up diapers, I'd get back to thinking and doing one thing at a time.

Now, a year later, my brain is at the computer, my body is at the gym, and my family is waiting for me at home.

So I'm frustrated, at first, as I pump. Then my buddy Jerry walks by. "Good going, skinny," he remarks, flashing a grin. Hmmm.

Looking up, I see her in the mirror: a not-so-bad-looking, middle-aged woman pumping iron. There's no evidence of inner angst, no sign of loose ends or half-baked quiches. Also no sign of skinny. However, the big weight in her hand is going up and down.

Incompletion, reflected back, looks remarkably complete.

Pausing, I take some notes for the book on my workout chart. I'll forget them, but it makes me feel better. Then I mark seventeen pounds for the bicep curl, my best. My weight, at 168 pounds, has not changed in eight months. Yet the Weight Watchers leader who lost 100 said every week you don't gain is a victory.

I return home to peals of laughter. "Daddy is telling a story!" Jessica says, running into the kitchen to announce the good news before bounding out again.

Bill's recitation of *The Lion King* is long and enchants, giving me time to record my thoughts, which have come full circle. Incompletion, I scribble, is actually an enlightened concept, the bit-by-bit approach the best way for a busy mom to get things done. It's messy, sometimes mind-boggling—but there's an efficiency to thinking of one thing while doing another. Didn't mystery writer and mother Agatha Christie say she got her best ideas while washing the dishes? The time-management experts themselves suggest breaking projects into small tasks.

And as Hemingway noted, there's an advantage to leaving the writer a bit hungry, eager to get back to the page. I may suffer from project interuptus, but I don't have writer's block. Staring at the computer, blankly? What a luxury! What a hoot!

If my brain is in one place and my body in another—well, it isn't very spiritual, but Jesus was childless, and the Buddha had to leave his wife and infant son to find enlightenment. I can't give up goals. With two kids, I need to set some sights to get halfway up the mountain. Yet few days are going to go according to plan; in these early years with a growing family, baby steps are more likely than great leaps forward. And the best advice is probably not going to come from the self-help gurus but from other parents like Gwen and Daisy.

Often we get the lives we want, with all their conflicts and competing claims. I want to be a writer. I want to be healthy. I could take more time from my kids to write about them, but that seems absurd. My various selves protest mightily at their restrictions. Yet, in fact, I have precisely the life that I want, with all its resulting chaos, competing claims, and unfinished business.

Last spring, as the crocuses poked their heads through the mud and the rain fell in torrents, my brother and I emptied three tons of my father's life into a Dumpster. All Dad's projects were finished, his to-do's complete.

I can live with incompletion.

Setting down the pen, my frustration subsides. It's been a busy week. My grand plan is history. My weight hasn't budged. I've increased my writing time by thirty minutes a day.

However, there's a quiche in the fridge, my biceps have a baby bulge, and though it's rough, another chapter is drafted. The magazine essay is revised. The preschool teachers have been thanked. My thoughts from the gym aren't as brilliant as they seemed without pen and paper, yet they're building blocks to something better. And if I'm still using half-and-half in my coffee, I've bagged the PB&J crusts.

Isabelle remembers her name. Jessica can distinguish Toot from Puddle.

Gwen hasn't finished the hallway.

But I know she will.

The Promised Land

It began the Easter before Jessica's third birthday when my younger dressed herself. Resurrection! Redemption! Praise the Lord! Without a little wiggle worm in my lap, I even heard the sermon. Later the egg hunt was unusually amusing. What was it? Then I realized: for the first time, I wasn't worrying about anyone choking on a jellybean.

The next milestone came in the pool. "I can't figure it out," I told Bill, shaking my head. "Swimming is so much more fun this year."

"That's because Jessica no longer needs the swim diaper," he pointed out. The swim diaper! How could I have forgotten? In the past my younger child had always pooped the minute her tush hit water. Swimming, for me, meant scrambling to peel off a poopy diaper before its contents leaked out, cleaning my arms, Jessica's legs, and the bathroom counter before putting her in a new one and praying that she was finished. Now, our little lady trotted off to the potty by herself. One small step for Jessica. One giant step for Mom.

The big breakthrough, however, came at the zoo. I've never liked zoos. I remember as a child watching smelly monkeys pick their fannies in cages and pleading to skip the reptile building. After my firstborn turned five, though, guilt set in. "Isabelle's never been to the zoo?" my aunt, a zoo volunteer, gasped, as if I regularly locked my child in a closet. Now, with Jessica out of diapers, it was time. A vivid description of the monkeys' antics got the girls in the car quickly. I didn't expect to have fun, but figured my kids would.

A few hours later, however, I had to pull myself away. Miami Metrozoo is a great attraction, with animals roaming in large, outdoor spaces on 740 acres of land. My girls' awed expressions watching the gorilla mom nurse her baby were worth the price of admission. As troop leader, I hurried them away from the reptile show without even a sidewise glance. And oh, the joy of passing the diaper changing table and slipping into separate big-girl stalls! We even walked all the way to the elephant and back without a single "Mommy! Up! Up!"

The zoo marked a breakthrough. Of course we'd had fun before, and I'd long ago learned to manage the kids. Things had been getting easier, in that two steps forward, one step back way that children's development works. Now, though, we'd embarked on a major adventure, diaper and stroller free without a hitch. Most remarkably, not only were the kids having fun, Mom was too.

I was still talking excitedly about the mama gorilla at dinner. "I thought you didn't like zoos," said Bill, mystified.

My husband didn't get it. But then, he hadn't burst into tears when the double stroller broke, irreparable.

"I didn't," I conceded. "Listen, though. Do you think we should buy the annual pass?"

When my kids were one and three, I asked a mother with older children also spaced two years apart when things got easier. Recalling myself as a new mother asking whether life would normalize at five or nine months, I hesitated to pose this question. If my first child had taught me anything, it was that there are few magic dates, children bringing a complete and irrevocable life change. However, Isabelle had just discovered the joys of "decorating" the house and Jessica was throwing shoe fits to rival Imelda Marcos. I felt desperate.

"Three and five," the mom answered without hesitation. "That's when they really start to play together, and you don't have to supervise them so closely."

With two years to go, this was not what I wanted to hear. But then, some date was better than none. And it was comforting to hear that my difficulties were universal. Queries to other moms confirmed it: three or so was the turning point. Jessica DeGroot, whose Third Path Institute in Philadelphia helps couples redesign their lives so both spouses can be primary parents and pursue meaningful careers, calls the phase in which any child is three or under the "new family stage." "Don't even expect life to be anything but hard with a child three or younger," DeGroot advised me when Jessica was two.

Well, okay—four and six were more realistic markers, but I couldn't wait that long, and mine were girls. My mantra became "Three and five." Isabelle wet her bed and Jessica was on her fourth week of diarrhea? "Three and five, three and five." Two toddlers were throwing tantrums in different rooms, each screaming for Mommy? "Three and five, three and five." "Om," "Nam-myoho-renge-kyo"—I tried those too. But "Three and five" worked best.

They say your younger child leads you out of the wilderness. A friend whose son took four years to potty train had to wait a long time. With her princess aspirations, however, Jessica learned to use the bathroom early and easily. Forced by my foot problems to walk on her own, she stopped insisting that I carry her at age two. Her shoe fetish continued through her third birthday. And Daddy's stern "Jessica, open your mouth" still rang through the house at teeth-brushing time. But when she blew out the three candles on the Snow White cake, the promised land was in sight.

Yet why didn't the other moms tell me? If I'd known, I would have sung my mantra instead of grimly reciting it.

Life isn't just easier with people who dress themselves and poop on the potty. It's divine.

So, what will it be? It's Saturday, and we're exploring our options. The zoo? Nope, been there, done that—three times in one holiday week alone, Mommy's enthusiasm having inspired Daddy too. Seaquarium? "Nah," says Isabelle. "We just saw the dolphins. How about Fairchild Tropical Garden?"

"Yes! Fairchild!" echoes Jessica, knowing nothing about the place, but ever the mimic.

Now, had I known that one day my children would be demanding to go to an enchanting tropical garden, Jessica's twos might actually have looked like a phase. Fairchild at my kids' insistence? Could this be?

There's a minor shoe meltdown, some fighting over which music to play in the car. However, Mommy having made clear that it's consensus or nothing and that they have to work it out themselves, my daughters quickly agree on a tape. (Thank you *Siblings Without Rivalry.)* All is serene as we drive to the gardens, for my first time in—can this be?—five years.

Without hesitation, I buy the annual pass. Isabelle leads me to the tram. As we ride, the driver names the exotic plants. At the café, we get off and walk to a pond brimming with white-flowered water lilies. "Let's pretend I am the mommy and you are the daughter," Isabelle tells her sister.

"And we are going up the mountain, then I fall," says Jessica, tumbling on the nearby grass and pulling big sister down. Locked in an embrace, a giggly bundle of flailing arms and legs rolls around.

I understand, now, that cliché that earlier sounded so nauseating: "It goes by so fast." After years of anticipating the next milestone, I want to stop here. I'd expected ages three and five to be easier, but hadn't imagined that it would be fun. Now, watching my girls play, I wonder if it will ever be so great again. As a mom, I've often wanted to freeze moments; if I never get to heaven, it's okay—I've experienced it on the carousel with Isabelle and Jessica. Now, though, I want to preserve an entire stage. I avoid the cliché, but its meaning rings in my note to a friend: "I want to freeze dry my kids at this age; they're just so cute."

From potty training and toddler tantrums, we've arrived smack dab in a magical era, and I don't want the show to end.

There are still many breakdowns, of course. Jessica recently took five outfits to the zoo ("just in case I want to change, Mommy"). And they still sometimes drive me nuts. More often, though, we can dress and leave without a major meltdown, eat dinner in a restaurant without one—or two—seeking Mommy's lap and spilling her drink, and even enjoy family outings. Fun has become almost predictable.

For three years, my kids' close spacing made parenting difficult. Now, it often makes things easier. With Jessica and Isabelle fast friends, I've got the perfect playdate for every occasion—no small advantage in a world where kids no longer frolic freely in their neighborhoods and Mom arranges every social encounter. Close in age, they enjoy the same things. If two toddlers "decorating" the house was hell, two ballerinas dancing in the kitchen is heaven.

So let me stop here, on this grassy spot where my girls roll in a giggly lovelock. Fun was one reason I wanted a bigger family. Let me mark the place where Mommy's dream came true. The homework years await, and driving, too. And two adolescent girls? I don't even want to think about it. From talking to parents with older children, I also know that some challenges, like finding time for romance or even conversation with your spouse, are ongoing.

For now, though, the big world is at bay. It's a mommy day, and the birds' chirping is punctuated by high-pitched squeals and giggles as Jessica and Isabelle tumble together.

It's not what I imagined during those early second-child conversations with Bill.

It's better.

AFTERWORD

Final Thoughts and a Flashback

"Two kids. Two C-sections," I whisper, giving my husband a little love jab as he peers into the jewelry case, wide-eyed.

Defying tradition, I didn't get a ring before we married. It didn't mean anything to me; I skipped the white dress too. Now, after eight years of marriage and two children, the ring reflects our proven commitment. Five years in maternity clothes, nursing dresses, and mommy warm-ups has made sparkly look pretty good too. A family of four, only one dented pot—it's a major marital accomplishment. Bill would have paid less if we'd gotten the ring earlier. But the man who agonizes about CD prices doesn't flinch.

I finally get an engagement ring.

It's been a long journey from those early second-child conversations to the jewelry counter. Yet the ring is symbolic, proof that a couple can survive the formative years of family life. With the kids three and five, Bill and I have launched our little brood, and our relationship is stronger than ever. The years of diaper duty and sleepless nights have passed. With homework just ahead, I have no illusions of reliving our newlywed days—more likely we're on a hiatus. Yet the fellow picking up Play-Doh is still the one I want to snag. If marriages suffer when dad doesn't do his domestic share, the converse is also true. No man is more appealing than a true parenting partner, especially as the family grows and the stakes increase.

As the ring shows, life beyond one continues to evolve, making an update of earlier themes helpful. Most changes have been positive. One evening after Jessica turned three, for instance, it simply happened: we all sat down for dinner together and even talked. Then we began eating together regularly. Our family meals are still often ad hoc and disorganized. But they're more enjoyable than I ever could have imagined during the food-throwing days. I even look forward to them.

Life has been easier with both kids in school. Jessica and Isabelle are up at seven, out at eight. The earlier schedule helps explain the ring. Now able to speak to my mate in the evenings, I no longer dream of divorce. With Jessica out sooner, I can work more too.

The earlier schedule has made routines even more essential. However, since writing "Creature of Habit," I've come to appreciate the old parenting adage that just when you figure things out, they change. Isabelle's Saturday tumbling class, for instance, proved a stroke of genius when I could tend Jessica quietly on the side. Run that preschooler! Roll her! Work her out! Then little sister became mobile and I began expending more energy keeping Jessica out of the class than Isabelle expended in it. What had worked perfectly no longer worked at all. Establishing an effective routine is only half the battle. You also have to know when to let it go.

And parents with kids rooming together take heart: once the little one stops napping you're over the hump. Getting the kids to bed has become much easier since Jessica gave up her siesta. Meanwhile, Bill and I still sleep happily apart. When I wrote "Sharing a Room," I thought we were an anomaly. Since then I've learned of other couples with the same arrangement. May my ring serve as proof that a little extra distance and shut-eye can make the heart grow fonder.

Challenges remain, of course. I've had it, for instance, with toddler meltdowns. By the time my younger daughter turns four this spring, I will have been living with Band-Aid and boo-boo fits for five years. Sure, it's a phase, but it's been longer than college. When I'm not wishing I could stop time, I'm pondering my graduation. We'd probably have fewer breakdowns if I'd follow my own advice, dispensed in "Bring in the Bears." Getting Jessica up for school by pretending to be a crane pulling her out of bed recently reminded me of the value of humor. Being outnumbered makes a mom far too serious. The next note on the fridge is going to read, "Be Absurd."

My projects remain incomplete. Big stuff, small stuff—it's never finished, nor, I remind myself, should it be. Yet this book is a testament to the bit-by-bit approach. The subtitle was written on an exercise chart. Many of the chapter themes emerged at the kitchen sink. I couldn't have written *Beyond One* without the blocks of time and peace of mind that Nancy's excellent childcare provides. Yet a lot was also squeezed into odd moments. Picking Isabelle up from school or packing the lunch box often unblocked my writing. Choreographer Twyla Tharp describes how movement spurs creativity in *The Creative Habit*. As a mommy writer, I've found shifting gears to be beneficial as often as it's distracting.

Simplicity remains elusive, despite my attempts to emulate Bill's example. The problem is now clear: a man's small stuff is a woman's life. Over the holidays Bill and I bickered about—of all things—wrapping paper. "Why don't you just put the presents out in their boxes?" my husband asked. Give me a break. I may have passed on the school wrapping-paper campaign, yet remembering my mother's festive Christmases, I carefully wrapped every barrette and Pooh pen. Simplifying remains a major mommy conundrum, far easier said than done. My choices surely make sense only to me.

Most difficult has been maintaining a social life. Work, children, and marriage leave little time for the dessert of life: friends. Three years after the birth of my second child, I'm still lonely in the crowd. I expected this. Though I hear of mommy book clubs, playgroups, and even retreats, and get lots of forwarded emails on the value of friendship, few mothers I know beyond one have much time to socialize. You can't "get a life" without friends, though, and this is my next frontier. There's reason for hope: I've finally almost grown into the book I bought prematurely years ago, *The Girlfriends' Guide to Getting Your Groove Back*. May the "mommy mole" hole, as Iovine calls it, be a phase. Girlfriends, don't give up on me!

~

If the second child makes Mommy an expert, time proves her wrong. On a couple of matters, I'm eating crow. Our new school raised $7,000 by selling wrapping paper(!). I don't know if this means that I should buy some, or enroll moms in a greater cause, like global warming, but it gives me pause. Meanwhile, every time Bounty sucks up a spill, I think of Marta.

Mostly, though, my earlier discoveries still hold, especially concerning siblings. Rivalry gets too much attention. Loyalty is at least as important. Last night big sister sobbed hysterically as I dug a thorn out of little sister's foot. "Mommy, please! Don't hurt Jessie!" Isabelle screamed, tears streaming down her face. The value of siblings becomes ever clearer as my brother Jon and I recover from the loss of our father, and my girls grow closer.

My best insight, though, remains my first: that a second child would bring my entire family great joy. That huge leap of faith made years ago with such trepidation now appears as one of my best decisions. Every choice involves trade-offs. I occasionally envy the freedom of mothers of one, and imagine an amazing third child. Yet two is right for me. Often, I look at Jessica and think: Thank God I had you. I mean, life without two princesses prancing down the hallway?

I can no longer imagine.

~

However, kids keep you focused on the present, tracking down the blankie. Rarely is perspective possible in a growing family.

So the old diary entry shocked me. I'd made it nine years earlier while visiting my niece and nephew, then ages two and four. After writing about how cute they were, I added: "Yet when I honestly look at myself, I don't think I have the energy for parenting. Certainly not for two. Two looks absolutely impossible."

Motherhood is a drip-drip process, the big picture obscured by pediatrician's appointments and missing shoes. Progress is especially hard to identify in the chaos beyond one. So often, in recent years, I've felt myself going backward instead of forward—all those stained nursing clothes and baby bibs reappearing from storage, and life unspooling past those first-baby standards.

I'm still not crazy about small children, but I seem to love a lot of people six and under. I wish I never yelled, yet I'm proud of my bear imitations.

And perhaps it's because of my shortcomings and hesitant start that when I do reflect, the miracle before me is so clear.

Sporting a smile as sparkly as her tutu, Isabelle pirouettes to Jessica's top-of-the-toddler-lungs rendition of "Twinkle, Twinkle Little Star."

A clan. Sisters. Siblings. A brood.

The impossible has become possible, right under my nose.

Introduction: Taking the Leap

Abrams, Rebecca. *Three Shoes, One Sock & No Hairbrush: Everything You Need to Know About Having Your Second Child.* United Kingdom: Cassell & Co., 2001. For an overview of studies on the impact of additional children on women's well-being.

Crittenden, Ann. *The Price of Motherhood: Why the Most Important Job in the World Is Still the Least Valued*. New York: Owl Books, 2002.

Diamant, Anita. *Pitching My Tent: On Marriage, Motherhood, Friendship and Other Leaps of Faith.* New York: Scribner, 2003.

Deutsch, Francine M. *Halving It All: How Equally Shared Parenting Works*. Cambridge: Harvard University Press, 2000.

Dunn, Judy. *From One Child to Two: What to Expect, How to Cope, and How to Enjoy Your Growing Family.* New York: Fawcett Columbine, 1995. For the finding that most siblings value their relationship both as older children and as adults.

—— and Carol Kendrick. *Siblings: Love, Envy, and Understanding*. Cambridge: Harvard University Press, 1982. For study noting deterioration of relations between the older sibling and the mother after a second child's birth.

Haas, Nancy. "We Are Family: Mom, Dad and Just Me," *The New York Times*, October 24, 1999. For prevalence of single-child families in Manhattan.

Hochschild, Arlie Russell. *The Second Shift*. New York: Avon Books, 1997. Latest reissue edition: Penguin USA, 2003. For an in-depth look at the devastating effect on marriage when Dad refuses to share domestic responsibilities after the birth of a second child.

Jong, Erica. *Fear of Fifty: A Midlife Memoir.* New York: HarperCollins, 1997. For those interested in stopping at one, Jong's memoir is also worth consulting. Notes the mother of one: "So I have made my choices and I am mostly glad of them. The intensity of one mother–one daughter sometimes makes me wish I had a household full of noisy kids, but the truth is I know now that even I, with all my prodigious energy, can't do everything."

Leonard, Joan. *Twice Blessed: Everything You Need to Know About Having a Second Child—Preparing Yourself, Your Marriage, and Your Firstborn for a New Family of Four*. New York: St. Martin's Griffin, 2000. For the second child's impact on marital relations.

Ralston, Jeannie. "How Many Kids Should We Have?" *Parenting*, September 2002. For research finding that women usually get their way on family size, as well as useful information for couples dealing with this issue.

Stewart, Robert B. Jr. *The Second Child: Family Transition and Adjustment*. Thousand Oaks: Sage Publications, 1990. For more results from his study of the impact of the second child on forty-one American couples, including the increased involvement of the father with the second child.

Upton, Rebecca L. "The Next One Changes Everything: Parental Adjustment to the Second Child Among Middle-

Class American Families." Working paper, The Center for the Ethnography of Everyday Life: An Alfred P. Sloan Center for the Study of Working Families, The University of Michigan, Ann Arbor, 2000.

Wiedemann, Katharina. "The Rise of the Only Child," *Newsweek International*, April 23, 2001. For a discussion of the increasing popularity of one-child families in developed nations, including statistics on their growth. The article notes that despite the popular stigma, "Study after study has found the same thing: whether they grow up in Thailand or Bolivia, only children are indistinguishable from those with siblings."

Room Service

Weiss, Joan Solomon. *Your Second Child: A Guide for Parents*. New York: Fireside, 1981. For research finding that women have more emotional problems and are more depressed with the second pregnancy.

Sex Preferences

Leonhardt, David. "It's a Girl! (Will the Economy Suffer?) Couples with Boys are Divorcing Less." *The New York Times*, October 26, 2003. For economists Gordon B. Dahl and Enrico Moretti's research finding that couples with girls divorce more often than those with boys, not just in developing countries such as China, but also in the United States.

Stewart, Robert B. Jr. *The Second Child: Family Transition and Adjustment*. Thousand Oaks: Sage Publications, 1990. For finding that nearly half of the mothers who'd initially wanted their second child to be a girl could not recall having stated such a preference or denied having done so.

Sibling Rivalry

Faber, Adele, and Elaine Mazlish. *Siblings Without Rivalry: How to Help Your Children Live Together So You Can Live Too*. New York: Avon Books, 1987. Expanded edition: Avon, 1998. For the sibling sanity savers I've cited, and more.

Lansky, Vicki. *Welcoming Your Second Baby*. Minnetonka, Minnesota: Book Peddlers, 1990. Revised edition: Book Peddlers, 2003.

Weiss, Joan Solomon. *Your Second Child: A Guide for Parents*. New York: Fireside, 1981. For research on the older child's doing better when the father is actively involved with her after the birth of a sibling and the finding that girls are more jealous than boys.

The Sex Police

Iovine, Vicki. *The Girlfriends' Guide to Getting Your Groove Back: Loving Your Family Without Losing Your Mind*. New York: Perigee, 2001.

Muscles and Wrapping Paper

Stewart, Robert B. Jr. *The Second Child: Family Transition and Adjustment*. Thousand Oaks: Sage Publications, 1990. For increased involvement of fathers after a second child arrives.

Creature of Habit

Stewart, Robert B. Jr. *The Second Child: Family Transition and Adjustment*. Thousand Oaks: Sage Publications, 1990. For mothers' hitting a low point when the second child reaches eight months and becomes mobile.

Double Up

Deutsch, Francine M. *Halving It All: How Equally Shared Parenting Works*. Cambridge: Harvard University Press, 2000. The notes to Deutsch's first chapter provide an analysis of studies that find stay-at-home mothers more depressed than those who work outside of the home, with the exception of full-time working mothers who get little help from their spouses.

Stewart, Robert B. Jr. *The Second Child: Family Transition and Adjustment*. Thousand Oaks: Sage Publications, 1990. For more on the stress of staying home with small children. Stewart found that women who were not working outside the home four months after their second child's birth experienced higher levels of stress associated with depression, social isolation, and marital problems than those who were.

The Amazing Toddler Diet

Weng, Haoling H., and others. "Number of Children Associated with Obesity in Middle-Aged Women and Men: Results from the Health and Retirement Study," *Journal of Women's Health* 13, No. 1 (2004): 85. For study finding that a woman's risk of obesity increases by 7 percent for each child she has, while men's goes up 4 percent.

Missing the Baby-Doll Gene

Jeffers, Susan. *I'm Okay, You're a Brat: Setting the Priorities Straight and Freeing You from the Guilt and Mad Myths of Parenthood*. Los Angeles: Renaissance Books, 2001.

Sharing a Room

Zweiback, Meg. *Keys to Preparing and Caring for Your Second Child*. New York: Barron's Educational Series, Inc., 1991. For a positive view of children's sharing a room.

It's a Phase

Dunn, Judy. *From One Child to Two: What to Expect, How to Cope, and How to Enjoy Your Growing Family*. New York: Fawcett Columbine, 1995. For the finding that neither birth order nor spacing has a critical effect on personality and adjustment.

White, Burton L. *The New First Three Years of Life*. New York: Fireside, 1995. For information on the difficulties that result from close spacing of children.

Breathe In, Breathe Out

Dunn, Judy, and Carol Kendrick. *Siblings: Love, Envy, and Understanding*. Cambridge: Harvard University Press, 1982. For study noting a striking rise in confrontation between mothers and firstborns after the birth of a second child.

Klass, Perri. "No More Yelling! The New Golden Rules of Discipline, from a Pediatrician Mom Who's Found Better Ways to Get Her Kids to Behave," *Parenting*, April 2004.

Severe, Sal. *How to Behave So Your Preschooler Will, Too*. New York: Penguin USA, 2004.

Spencer, Paula. "Old Yeller: The Surprising Benefits of Raising Your Voice to Your Child," *Parenting*, June 2002

ACKNOWLEDGMENTS

I'm grateful to Ingrid Emerick, who came up with the idea for this book during her second pregnancy. Having an editor with personal experience in your subject can be a blessing or a curse. In this case, it's definitely been a blessing. May you, dear Ingrid, reach the promised land with your little ones too.

Ingrid contacted me after reading "Sweet Silence" in *Brain, Child* magazine. Thanks to Jennifer Niesslein and Stephanie Wilkinson, the editors of that fine publication, as well as to Linda Rodgers at *Parenting* and Camille Peri at *Salon* for publishing my early essays on motherhood.

I'm indebted to all the friends who kept me sane and shared their wisdom, including Kathleen McAuliffe, Joann Biondi, Jeanne Dequine, Nicole Meske, Chris Spaulding, Anne Wallis, and the founding members of my baby group: Barbara Drake, Jen Karetnick, and Sara Reilly. And to my remaining Miami writer friends: I guess I *was* on the verge of something. Here it is. I hope to see much more of you now that it's done.

Nancy Barahona's excellent care of our children blesses our entire family. We love you, Nancy! St. Philip's Episcopal School and Church and the Miami Friends Meeting help make this big city feel small. And the folks at the Coral Gables Congregational Church Early Childhood Center are all angels.

My wonderful mother-in-law, Elaine Artoe, bought the double stroller and such beautiful clothes for our first daughter that we had to have a second. My good friend Beth Blatt got me into this whole business in the first place by introducing me to her brother. Perfect timing, Beth. I would never have gotten beyond the hair and thick glasses if you'd introduced us in high school.

Thanks to my cousin, Gwen Oelerich, for serving as a sounding board and inspiring the chapter "Incompletion." The hallway looks terrific!

My brothers are so great, I had to try for a second child. Jon Hull and Steve Pope are living proof of the value of siblings. And my relationship with Numo Jaeger shows that no matter how much the adults screw up, sisterly ties endure.

Give a kid enough pens and pads of paper, and it has an effect. My father, Morton Hull, continues to inspire my writing, now from on high. Meanwhile, my stepfather, Bill Pope, remains my buddy in the here and now.

My mother, Deede Pope, never read a parenting book, relying instead on common sense, love, and discipline to do an excellent job raising three children. Thanks, Mom, for making 10,000 peanut butter–and-jelly sandwiches, tending 5,000 boo-boos, making no mean no and yes mean yes, and being way cooler than the other mothers.

And to Bill Blatt: had I known that you make such beautiful babies and edit, I would have married you earlier. The nine P.M. revisions were tough, but I'm grateful for your extensive help and encouragement. Eight years of marriage, two kids, and one book later, I'm still crazy about you.

Finally, to Isabelle and Jessica: May your dreams come true too. Like I told you girls last night . . .

I *do* believe in fairies. I do! I do!

About the Author

Jennifer Bingham Hull has a master's degree in journalism and was a staff writer for both *The Wall Street Journal* and *Time* magazine. She is currently a freelance writer and has contributed to such publications as *The Atlantic Monthly*, *Parenting*, *Working Mother*, *Salon.com*, *Ms.*, *Los Angeles Times Magazine*, and *The Christian Science Monitor.* She lives in Coral Gables, Florida, with her husband and two daughters and can be contacted at www.jenniferhull.com.

SELECTED TITLES FROM SEAL PRESS

The Essential Hip Mama: Writing from the Cutting Edge of Parenting edited by Ariel Gore. $14.95, 1-58005-123-5. Hilarious and heart-wrenching essays from the coveted alternative parenting magazine *Hip Mama* are collected in this best-of-the-best anthology.

Mother Shock: Loving Every (Other) Minute of It by Andrea J. Buchanan. $14.95, 1-58005-082-4. One new mom's refreshing and down-to-earth look at the birth of a mother.

Toddler: Real-life Stories of Those Fickle, Irrational, Urgent, Tiny People We Love edited by Jennifer Margulis. $14.95, 1-58005-093-X. These clever, succinct, and poignant tales capture all the hilarity, magic, and chaos of raising the complex little people we call toddlers.

Whatever, Mom: Hip Mama's Guide to Raising a Teenager by Ariel Gore. $15.95, 1-58005-089-1. Hip Mama's back—dispensing wisdom, humor, and common sense to parents who've been dreading the big 1-3 (or counting the days until 1-8).

The Big Rumpus: A Mother's Tales from the Trenches by Ayun Halliday. $15.95, 1-58005-071-9. Creator of the wildly popular *East Village Inky*, Halliday describes the quirks and everyday travails of a young urban family, warts and all.

Growing Seasons: Half-baked Garden Tips, Cheap Advice on Marriage, and Questionable Theories on Motherhood by Annie Spiegelman. $14.95, 1-58005-079-4. A celebration of family in all its comfort and complexity.